medKnitation

medKnitation

30 Meditations for Knitting, Crochet,
and Spiritual Stitching

SUZAN COLÓN

WINDING ROAD STORIES

NEW YORK   LOS ANGELES

Jacket design by Rejenne Pavon
Jacket Copyright © 2024 by Winding Road Stories
Interior Design by A Raven Design
Interior Illustrations by Suzan Colón
ISBN#: 978-1-960724-44-1 (pbk)
ISBN#: 978-1-960724-45-8 (ebook)

Published by Winding Road Stories
www.windingroadstories.com

PRAISE FOR MEDKNITATION

I love this book. The idea of pairing handwork with meditation is lovely. Suzan Colón is so honest, like a friend right there beside us: she shares her life with us even as she provides us with a series of guided meditations to use for pretty much any situation. Her decades of experience with meditation are on full display here—she wants us to discover the peace that comes with the simple act of slowing down for a few moments. This is a book I will keep by my computer, to return to again and again, as a respite from all the things inside my computer!

— ANN SHAYNE, CO-FOUNDER OF *MODERN DAILY KNITTING*

I know firsthand how knitting has actually saved me, comforting me through tough times, helping with anxiety and boosting creativity. But learning that knitting could also be meditative was revelatory for me. Here, Suzan Colón's wise, inspiring book offers up a way of stitchery that I had never considered—one that's spiritual, intentional, and transformational. I loved each of these 30 meditations because they not only changed my knitting—they changed me.

— CAROLINE LEAVITT, NEW YORK TIMES BESTSELLING AUTHOR OF *PICTURES OF YOU* AND *DAYS OF WONDER*

I had the pleasure of meeting Suzan Colón many years ago at Knitty City. It was there that Suzan first introduced me to how knitting and meditation can be used as helpful tools in achieving balance and calm. I know firsthand the healing and restorative power of knitting, as I was able to use the rhythmic motions of knitting to conquer my fear of flying as well as to gently move through the grief process of losing close family members. In *medKNITation*, Suzan adds structure and intentionality to the already mindful practice of knitting. Through her 30 guided meditations, Suzan masterfully connects these practices, demonstrating their positive impact on mental health and emotional well-being. Her work speaks to the transformative power of creativity combined with mindfulness.

— **CECILIA NELSON-HURT, DIVERSITY & INCLUSION PRACTITIONER, VOGUE KNITTING DIVERSITY ADVISORY BOARD**

Suzan Colón explores two of her passions—knitting and meditation—and seamlessly combines them to offer knitters and crocheters another layer to the wellness benefits of these fiber arts crafts. In addition to explaining why knitting is meditative, Colón has a way of demystifying meditation to make it easily approachable, even for a novice. This book is jam-packed with easy-to-follow meditation practices, providing a toolkit for knitters who want to deepen their knitting experience.

— **CAROL CAPAROSA, FOUNDER, PROJECT KNITWELL**

OTHER BOOKS BY SUZAN COLÓN

Cherries in Winter:
My Family's Recipe for Hope in Hard Times

Yoga Mind: Journey Beyond the Physical
30 Days to Enhance Your Practice and
Revolutionize Your Life from the Inside Out

Beach Glass: A Novel

CONTENTS

FOREWORD

In a world where the pace of life can often feel overwhelming, Suzan Colón's *medKNITation* stands out as a beacon of calm and introspection for fiber artists and anyone seeking solace. This self-guided meditation book offers thirty unique meditations, each tailored to help us navigate the complexities of our emotions and daily challenges.

One of the aspects I cherish most about *medKNITation* is Suzan's openness, honesty, and transparency. Through sharing her own personal stories and journeys, she creates a deep connection with readers, making each meditation feel both intimate and universal. While reading it, I felt as though I was sitting with a friend. Whether you are grappling with anxiety, fear, heartbreak, or simply seeking a moment to appreciate the world around you, this book provides a powerful tool to address personal struggles and hurdles.

Some of my favorite medKNITations include "Meet This Day," a gentle reminder to embrace the present; "Patience," which teaches us to be gentle with ourselves and others; "Compassion," which fosters empathy; and "Closure," helping us find peace with past experiences.

Suzan's short affirmations are another highlight of this book. They serve as quick, uplifting reminders that can be integrated into daily life. Two of my favorite affirmations are "My kindness can change someone's day," and "I am learning, growing, and evolving every day." These simple yet profound statements encapsulate the essence of medKNITation and its transformative potential.

medKNITation is not just for fiber artists; it's a must-read for everyone. As a bonus, Suzan also guides us through Yoga movements specifically designed for yarn lovers, adding an extra layer of mindfulness and physical well-being to our practice.

Working in education, I am particularly inspired to incorporate the "Kindness Hearts Project" with the children at my school (a project started by Suzan). I believe that teaching young minds the importance of kindness and mindfulness can have a lasting positive impact, and Suzan's work provides an excellent foundation for this initiative.

Suzan Colón's *medKNITation* is more than a book; it's a journey into mindfulness and self-compassion. I am certain it will become a cherished resource for many, just as it has for me.

Louis Boria
Brooklyn Boy Knits
July 2024

PART I
THE GIFT OF MEDKNITATION

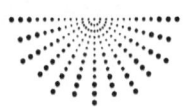

INTRODUCTION: CASTING ON

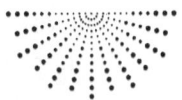

Do fifteen minutes of knitting every day; it will change your life.

— PEARL CHIN, FOUNDER OF KNITTY CITY, NEW
YORK CITY, NY

There's a lot to love about knitting. You get to hold soft, fuzzy yarn in your hands. The colors of yarn are uplifting, joyful. And, with the help of what amounts to a long string of spun fiber and a set of sticks, you weave something where, moments ago, there was nothing. Knitting is magic. I knit because I love all those things, but mostly, I knit because I need it.

The true magic of knitting can't be seen. People who knit—who love the craft so much they don't say "I knit," but rather, "I'm a knitter"—are aware of this essential sparkle. Even if they aren't conscious of it, they agree there's something special about weaving by hand in an age when you can get a sweater or a scarf in a single click. I knew nothing about this secret magic of weaving fiber, and how knitting can weave the weaver together, until my life was falling apart.

3

At the start of what looked like a glorious summer, a friend had a diving accident that left him paralyzed. Not long after that, another dear friend was diagnosed with terminal cancer. Right around that time, the magazine I'd been working for shut down and I lost my job. I barely had a moment to take a breath when an on-again, off-again relationship I was in switched to the off position, permanently. That winter, in an almost comical dash of added tragedy, my sweet cat of nineteen years, Ethel, crossed the rainbow bridge.

At that point, I didn't even want to pick up the phone anymore, afraid of more bad news. But a friend called and mentioned that she was taking knitting lessons; did I want to come with her? I'd never given knitting much thought, but being able to think about anything other than what was happening at the time sounded darn good to me.

Our lessons took place in a tiny yarn shop not far from where I lived in Murray Hill, a small neighborhood in Manhattan. I walked up a flight of carpeted stairs and straight into coziness: shelves filled with plush balls of yarn in muted autumnal tones, brighter skeins looped around wooden pegs on the walls. Susan, our teacher, was soft-spoken, kind, and above all, patient. With her help, my friend and I learned to laugh at our mistakes.

Sitting in that yarn shop, working with bright orange yarn the color of cheerfulness, I felt my shoulders begin to relax. The knot of tension trying to protect my battered heart eased loose, and I took a deep breath. For the first time in months, I smiled.

Knitting, I thought, *is magic.*

As a longtime Yoga and meditation practitioner and teacher, I know the technical terms for this magic. During all the emotional turmoil, my sympathetic nervous system, also known as the stress response, was in high gear and on alert. My body's ancient wisdom was preparing me to fight or flee, though neither option was the answer to being fired or getting dumped. (The depression I was mired in had its own physical manifestations, such as a lowered immune system and a constant feeling of exhaustion.)

I knew that Yoga and meditation could help the sympathetic nervous system switch to the parasympathetic nervous system, the "peace response." Breathing would deepen, blood pressure would slow down, heart rate would return to normal, and stress hormones would stop flooding my body, allowing non-emergency functions such as digestion and immunity to resume. Overall, I would feel calmer and be healthier. Yet there was only so much Yoga I could do, and meditation sometimes brought the events that were upsetting me into sharper relief. I needed something else.

I didn't know what that was until I started knitting. At first, I fumbled through trying to make stitches, though that in itself was good meditative training: talk about focus. Once I could do the basic stitches, I found that knitting had the same soothing, grounding effect that Yoga and meditation gave me. (Not as much exercise, but nothing is perfect!)

In addition to that calm, meditative state, knitting felt joyful. Knitting is something that's done in today's automated, high-tech world for pure pleasure. In one of the guided meditations in this book, you'll see that knitting has many of the elements that bring on a joyful state. If you knit, you know: Knitting is one of the few things that can be done almost anywhere, that feels good in your hands, that produces something tangible, sharable, and made with love, and that promotes feelings of happiness, relaxation, and satisfaction.

Knitting is magic, but its benefits are scientifically measurable and proven. Knitting is a bona fide stress reduction technique, one that can bring on the same health and mental wellbeing benefits as traditional forms of meditation. For people who find meditation challenging, knitting is more a more accessible, and enjoyable, way to relieve stress.

That is, when knitting is done as a form of meditation. Which, as I found out, it usually isn't. We live in an age of distraction. Never before has our attention been pulled in so many directions. The busyness of our lives is compounded by screens flashing information almost everywhere we go—especially the small screens we carry all the time, our phones. They ping, beep, buzz, and ring for our attention, a constant source of interruption and distraction.

The makers of social media and apps know our attention spans mean money for advertisers, and they invest multi-millions of dollars to make sure we become addicted, in a very real neurological sense, to our devices, and their apps. The result is that our ability to focus has become shorter and narrower. (You may have noticed that movies and TV shows mimic the speed of social media, with cuts every few seconds. Even pop music songs are getting shorter.) We never really have a chance to relax, to contemplate, to have a complete conversation or follow a train of thought without the phone interrupting, or the feeling that we must check our email, texts, or social media.

Another source of distraction is multitasking. In our parents' and grandparents' time, the ability to focus on a single task and do it well was considered a good work ethic. Today, we feel that if we're not juggling multiple tasks, we're not being productive. Work studies have proven that the more we do simultaneously, the less well we do each thing, yet we've gotten used to doing several things at a time. It's not unusual for people to check social media and text while watching TV —and knitting.

Knitting is, and always has been, relaxing, even in times when people made garments due to necessity. Now, knitting is generally done while doing something else, such as watching movies, talking with friends, having some wine at a knitting party, or all of the above at the same time. All of which is fun! Knitting is a great social activity. I love knitting with friends, and while my husband Nathan and I watch TV. But none of that is the same as knitting as a form of meditation.

As a Senior Editor at *O, the Oprah Magazine*, I was the first to read Ms. Winfrey's interviews with world-renowned spiritual leaders: The Dalai Lama, Pema Chödrön, Eckhart Tolle, Thich Nhat Hanh. Each of these thoughtful conversations emphasized the importance of cultivating inner peace through the process of meditation.

That process isn't always easy. As a Yoga and meditation instructor, I've heard many students, as well as friends and people in casual conversation, say "I can't meditate." (You may be saying it right now!) Some people don't know how, or, even if they learned one of the many meditation techniques available, they still felt they were doing it wrong. Others simply found it difficult to sit still and focus. Many people think that meditation means stopping all thoughts (not possible, a myth I dispelled in my book *Yoga Mind*), which is frustrating. There are also people who find meditation to be more stressful than calming.

In my Yoga training, I'd been taught not to ask people to do poses that might not be physically accessible to them, but instead to adapt Yoga to their individual needs. I wondered why meditation should be any different; if someone found traditional methods frustrating or stressful, why not give them a different way to meditate?

I knew that knitting was not only relaxing, but also meditative. I began to do research to see if any studies backed up my personal experience. There were very few—knitting isn't high on the health industry's radar for well-being—but I did find one study by a well-respected doctor who had seen firsthand what knitting could do for his patients. His interview in this book may be one of the most meaningful, even important things you ever read.

Bolstered by this doctor's information, I combined the meditation techniques I'd learned with knitting, creating a set of simple steps—a pattern, if you like—for a calming, grounding, stress-reducing experience. This is medKNITation.

I started teaching medKNITation at my favorite yarn shop, Knitty City, on Manhattan's upper west side, at the invitation of Pearl Chin, Knitty City's founder. Small groups of people came, not sure what this knitting meditation thing was all about, but willing to try it. These knitters already thought knitting was meditative; I wasn't sure I'd be telling them anything new.

But at the end of that first session, the room was full of happy smiles, relaxed shoulders, and looks of surprise. These seasoned knitters said, "I could've stayed in that meditation all night!" "Can I feel this way all the time?" and "When can we do this again?" Pearl set up monthly medKNITation sessions. People returned again and again, laughing about how they used to think they "couldn't meditate."

Then, as I led them through the medKNITation pattern, the room would become quiet, each person going on their own peaceful inner journey.

A few months later, I got a call from Vogue Knitting Live, the organization that hosts the largest gathering of knitters in the country. At first, I thought it was a joke, and it turned out they weren't too sure about it either. "We hear you do some kind of knitting meditation?"

I told them how knitting had become a form of meditation for me, and that I'd spoken with one of the lead researchers of a famous study about the effects of knitting, and about the monthly medKNITation sessions. "Great!" I heard, before I was even finished. "You're booked for Vogue Knitting Live in New York this January."

For nine years running, the Marriott Marquis Hotel in the heart of Times Square had been transformed into a knitting, crocheting, spinning, weaving, stitching, fiber-loving town. The event in January 2020 was the tenth anniversary of Vogue Knitting Live New York, so it would likely be even bigger. Still, a lecture about meditating by knitting? I figured maybe eight people would show up.

After online registration went live, Gabby, my contact at VKL, informed me that they'd be moving me to another room. "A smaller one?" I asked, imagining a broom closet with three chairs. "No, bigger," she said. A few weeks later, she told me I was going from a lecture room to a ballroom: one hundred and sixty people had signed up.

I brought cookies to the event, figuring that no one can be too disappointed if you give them sweets. I also crocheted one hundred and sixty small pink hearts to give to the participants. Making those hearts was so relaxing, I kept going, eventually making and giving away over four hundred Kindness Hearts throughout the event. (To date, I've made and given away a few thousand Kindness Hearts. You can find out more about them at the end of the book.)

When the day of the VKL event came, I gave a talk that is a condensed version of the book you're holding. Then it was time to find out if this "medKNITation" thing would work on a larger scale than ever before.

At the end, there were sighs of relief and smiles. I was amazed.

Over one hundred and sixty people, meditating in the heart of the busiest city in the world! That's the magic of knitting.

After the event, a long line of stitchers wanted to talk to me. One told me she'd known for years that knitting helped with her anxiety, but no one had ever affirmed that for her until that day. Now, she said, she would enjoy her knitting even more, knowing that there was actual proof that it was helpful. Two other knitters spoke to me of their adult children, who were in recovery for addiction started by over-prescription of opioid painkillers; did I think medKNITation would work for them? I didn't have the expertise to say for sure, but I encouraged these parents to try teaching their children to knit and crochet. When people are anxious, having something to work with in their hands can help them focus. This has been affirmed time and again by parents who have passed along the skill to children of any age and who have seen the gratifying, stress-relieving results. Also, a special bond is formed between teacher and student, whether family, friend, or perfect stranger. Once someone gives you the gift of knitting, you never forget them.

Others who'd come to the medKNITation event at Vogue Knitting Live said they hadn't felt this relaxed in ages, that they wanted to make this a regular practice, that they'd never been able to do traditional forms of meditation before, but that this could work for them. I saw that this didn't have to be a one-time event, and it could—and should —continue, in various ways. I've led medKNITation at other Vogue Knitting Live events, and at Virtual Knitting Live, the online version of VKL; I've taught knitting to hospital workers and psychiatrists as a stress-reduction technique for their patients and themselves; I've recorded a guided audio medKNITation; and now, I've written this book of guided medKNITations for you.

I've heard many people tell me that they've been knitting for years, and some that they've been meditating for years, but that medKNITation is different. People have said this is a simple, accessible way to ease into a meditative state. Others have told me that medKNITation helped with their anxiety and that they finally had a way to meditate that worked for them. At least one person has said, "medKNITation changed my life."

This is the true magic of knitting, and I want to share it with you.

Even though people say that the main reason they knit, crochet, or stitch is because it's so meditative, they still love learning why knitting works as a form of meditation, and the steps that turn their knitting into a true meditation practice. In the next chapter, the doctor who led a groundbreaking research study explains why knitting can be so beneficial. Read it, and you will feel forever empowered by knitting and fiber arts.

Then, in Section 2: The Guided medKNITations, you'll find the Basic medKNITation "Pattern." It's easy to become familiar with those simple steps, and then you'll be able to naturally fall into them, like working with a favorite pattern. After that, you'll find a series of guided medKNITations with themes that have become favorites at live and virtual medKNITation sessions, as well as new ones exclusive to this book.

You can practice these knitting meditations in a variety of ways:

- Do a month-long medKNITation challenge. Set aside time each day for a fifteen, ten, or even five-minute medKNITation. Ask friends or your knitting group to do this with you, either together in person or by yourselves. (I've found that doing anything with a partner or a group means I'm more consistent with it, even if we're doing it remotely. Plus, it's more fun!)
- While doing this as a challenge, keep a journal of how you feel at the beginning and end of the challenge, and on each day. That way, you can see what works for you and do more of that.
- Do the medKNITations in order, or look at the list of medKNITations in the Table of Contents and choose the one that resonates with you on a particular day.
- Pick a medKNITation and practice that one for a day, a few

days, even a week. You can do that with any medKNITation that speaks to you at a given time.

People who spin, weave, quilt, and sew by hand have told me that medKNITation works with those fiber arts too, so once you learn the steps, you can apply them to your craft of choice. I knit and crochet, but for the sake of brevity, I use the term "knitting" as shorthand for stitching of all kinds throughout the book. (I've been asked which I prefer, knitting or crochet, and I can't pick a favorite! Sometimes I gravitate toward the orderly, back-and-forth stitching of knitting, and when I need to release anxious energy, I go for the more energetic motion of crochet.)

Once you try medKNITation, you'll feel the benefits. And once you feel the benefits, you'll want to make medKNITation a regular practice. medKNITation in the morning is a relaxing way to start your day, and at night, medKNITation is a way to unwind from the day.

Pearl Chin, owner of Knitty City, had a wonderful saying: "Do knitting for fifteen minutes a day; it will change your life." Anyone who has been knitting, crocheting, or stitching knows about the blissful peace that can come when we set aside quiet time to weave. I believe we all need that quiet time in our lives, especially now.

medKNITation is about doing something necessary and wonderful: creating quiet time and space to sit, breathe, and just *be*. Intentionally setting aside time to recalibrate and regain your inner peace can have profound results for you, the people around you, and beyond. I've been amazed by the effects of medKNITation for myself and for others.

This book is here for you as a companion to creating that blissful, peaceful stillness through stitching. Who knows where it will take you, and what it can do for you and others?

Let's find out.

THE STORY BEHIND THE STUDY: WHY KNITTING IS MEDITATIVE

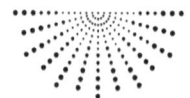

If you were in one of my Yoga classes and I instructed you to stand on one leg in Tree pose, you might do it, but you'd probably feel a little silly, standing like a wobbly tree. If I told you, "By doing this pose, you're strengthening the muscles of the leg you're standing on; you're building bone mass, which declines as we get older; and you're improving your balancing skills, which also decline with age," I bet you'd be a more enthusiastic about being a tree, even a wobbly one.

You may already know that knitting and other stitchwork is relaxing, but *why* is it relaxing? How does it have all these mental, physical, emotional, and even spiritual benefits? There's a theory that the benefits of health practices and treatments improve when people know why and how they work. When my Yoga students knew why and how the poses worked, they did them more mindfully and with more enthusiasm, and it's possible that the physical and mental benefits were increased. Based on that theory, this may be the most important chapter you read in this book.

While doing research on the ways knitting can affect people, I came across numerous mentions of a study showing that a group of patients diagnosed with anorexia nervosa reported feeling calmer during and after knitting lessons. Almost any article about the benefits of stitching would reference this study—but not how it worked. Why did knitting help these patients, and how did the researchers decide to choose knitting as part of a treatment for an eating disorder?

The phrase "studies have shown" has been so overused, usually with so little factual backup, that none of us at the *Oprah* Magazine could include it in an article without producing the name of the study, the statistics, and solid quotes from the researchers who'd conducted the study. When I kept seeing this particular study mentioned in articles about the benefits of knitting, yet without the details on the how and why, I looked up the original paper and emailed one of the lead researchers on the team to find out.

C. Laird Birmingham, MD, MHSc, FRCPC, FACP, ABIM, FAED, is a specialist in internal medicine, an epidemiologist, and a biostatistician, and he is Professor of Psychiatry at the University of British Columbia. Dr. Birmingham was in charge of the eating disorder clinic at St. Paul's Hospital in Canada, treating a group of people diagnosed with a variety of eating disorders, mostly anorexia nervosa. This is where the knitting study took place.

Though in high demand for his treatment of a variety of illnesses using Loreta Neurofeedback, Dr. Birmingham was kind enough to do a lengthy phone interview with me to discuss this study and the power, and potential, of knitting.

Suzan Colón: Dr. Birmingham, thank you for speaking with me. To get some background, the study you conducted says that anxious preoccupation with control of eating, weight, or shape is part of what inhibits recovery from anorexia. Would it be fair to say that this is similar to obsessive thinking?

Dr. Birmingham: It would have before, but I published an article showing where anorexia nervosa [AN] is in the brain. A lot of people don't know about it, but it's more like a phobia, an aversion circuit in the brain. Going along with any phobia is preoccupation, or obsession.

I've been studying AN for forty years, and patients who have it wake up in this preoccupation in the morning, have it all day, and go to bed with it. Obsession, rumination with something aversive—"aversive" is key. I've switched my treatment over the last several years to treat the brain. I do 3-D imaging of brain neural feedback treatment. It always involves the amygdala and insula, the parts of the brain concerning unconscious fear.

Is it similar to the kind of obsessive thinking addicts and alcoholics are prone to?

Obsessive thinking can be about almost anything. Addiction is in a different part of the brain, the pleasure centers, not in the aversive part of the brain.

Are there any findings about why this is the case with AN?

Yes, we know more about that now. In most cases of AN, there is a genetic predisposition, one that is polygenic—not one gene, but more than one. We believe this came down from caveman times, women who were able to survive periods of starvation.

AN can happen due to brain trauma, tumors, and post-infection inflammation, but in most cases, it's genetic. Like many genetic diseases, it needs something to activate it. For example, asthma, which I have, is genetic. I didn't show signs of having asthma until I was twenty-seven; I was allergic to cats, I got married at twenty-seven, my wife had a cat. The asthma was there genetically, but there needed to be something to cause it to happen. In many people predisposed to diabetes, there has to be weight gain around the middle to trip it.

AN requires weight loss. That weight loss needn't be due to dieting; it could be weight loss due to illness or an operation. If patients with a genetic predisposition to AN lose about 15 to 20 lbs. for any reason, the aversion starts, and it never goes away.

I hasten to add: Just as my asthma can't be cured, but can be controlled, AN can't be cured, but it can be controlled. It's not a question of cure versus no cure. Patients with AN can live with it if they can control the preoccupation.

How did knitting come into the eating disorder treatment program?

One of the people who worked there noticed the effect knitting had and thought we should try it. The thing I can take credit for is listening to people's suggestions [*laughs*]. Rebecca Park at Oxford, who was in the [study] article, had done MRIs that showed anxiety decreased when patients were knitting. That didn't solve the issue as to why knitting.

What I came to believe based on EMDR [*Eye Movement Desensitization and Reprocessing, a form of psychotherapy treatment*] is that you have to use both sides of the brain, left and right, to reduce the anxiety and the preoccupation. You can't use one side of the brain. Usually, EMDR is used for post-traumatic stress disorder. You're taking away anxiety by stimulating both sides of the brain at the same time. Then it becomes like having a wall, or a fog, between you and the problem; you can't see it as well. I became interested in this for anybody with anxiety, Asperger's, all kinds of anxiety-related issues. With knitting, you use both hands.

What about other hand-related activities?

I tried worry beads, which have been used around the world forever. I told the patients to use both hands and count; you can count subconsciously, but you have to move the beads through both hands. However, you end up with the dominant hand doing most of the work and the other hand not as much.

Sewing, painting, drawing, photography, they didn't work, I think because only one side of the brain is used at a time. Then there wasn't the cloud between the patients and whatever they're obsessively thinking about. Both sides of the brain need to be attentive to something in order for the thoughts to be not aversive. Because knitting used both hands, both sides of the brain were at work, so the desired affect was achieved.

The other major benefit of knitting is that you can still take part in conversation while you're doing it, whereas with painting or taking pictures, you can't really talk and do your work. I had a student who knit for the first two years of my medical school class; she could knit, listen, and converse. If she had been drawing, she couldn't have done that. Even though knitting is a habitual action [*an action that occurs repeatedly*], it uses both sides of the brain, and the level of anxiety is then decreased.

One could calm the patients' anxiety with drugs, but with knitting, the patients were attentive during therapy. They were able to listen, take in information, and converse while knitting. It was amazing! As far as I know, knitting is the only thing you can do that allows you to be totally involved in a conversation at the same time.

The third major thing we found was that patients loved that they were actually producing something—something for a child, a baby blanket, a hat, a scarf. There's a purpose to it. They're generally very proud of the things they knit.

How did you start working in the study of AN and eating disorders?

I studied in Toronto for internal medicine. I was interested in psychiatry, and I worked with some people treating weight and eating disorders, psychiatry, biofeedback. I was asked by the psychiatrists I'd worked with to take over an eating disorder clinic. I found it fascinating, but there was almost no research on the kind of work I do. We ended up having fifty-five people on the team, and I've written about two hundred and eighty articles on eating disorders by now. I was one of the first to show that warming the patients gets them better faster—yes, actually warming up their bodies. That's why many eating disorder treatment centers are in hot climates, and why there's less AN in hot climates.

This sounds like fascinating work, but it must be heartbreaking as well.

Oh, it is. I used to count the number of people I worked with who died. I got to thirty-seven and stopped. I decided to take it as not that we lost the patients, but rather that we helped them as much as we could and gave them a good quality of life. A patient's mother came to the ward and told me that even though her daughter had died, she knew she had received every kind of treatment available. If we're doing the best we can, everything we can, that helps.

The patients and their families are so happy that this work is going on. Even this work on knitting, a lot of people pooh-pooh it, but I don't know why it isn't used more widely. Sure, you could give marijuana to control anxiety in patients, but knitting is a lot better to do than that. There's your headline: Knitting is the New Marijuana!

I'll keep that in mind {*laughs*}. Who taught the patients in the study how to knit?

We had an occupational therapist who was working with us. She taught all the patients initially, but after a while, the patients started teaching one another, and teaching the new patients who came into the program. We gave them free lessons and access to supplies.

Did you provide yarn colors based on the idea that color has an effect on mood?

I had nothing to do with selecting the supplies, but I do know most patients had their own color preferences. Color does have an effect on mood, for sure. The colors that were used depended on what they were knitting and the season, things like that.

Were you with the patients at the time or observing from a distance?

I generally wouldn't be in the room; I didn't want the patients to be concerned about me seeing them learning to knit. I walked past from time to time. After they learned, it became more automatic, and they would be knitting in groups. They'd be more present and calmer.

This research took place in a hospital on a small island. When I'd to go back to the mainland on the ferry, I'd see the people who were working with me all knitting on the ferry. That told me something.

Wait—your colleagues started knitting too?

Everybody at the residential treatment center ended up knitting. Not only the patients—the staff, everyone. The staff saw the effect it had on the patients, how they calmed right down, and they wanted to try it too.

Did you learn to knit as well?

[*Laughs*] I didn't! I'm a bit of a klutz that way. I played the piano, which, if you play with both hands, engages both sides of the brain.

The study says, "Preliminary outcome requires further controlled study in AN subjects." Did the lessons in this clinic continue?

I don't know. The clinic was taken over by the government, and the occupational therapist and most of the other people were let go. When something is taken over by the government, they minimize staff and such.

Do you know if knitting has been used in other eating disorder clinics?

I don't, but I would imagine it has at the clinic in Oxford, because Rebecca Park was involved in our study. I have had calls from all over, as far away as Italy, so people are interested, but whether they're able to move past the naysayers who say it's not scientific, I don't know. There's lot of difficulty in trying to convince people to try new things in treatment. And if there's a drug they can come up with to sell, they want to use that.

However, I use knitting in the treatment of other psychiatric disorders now, like Asperger's Syndrome. Some patients with Asperger's do this thing called stimming, or stimulating [*hand flapping, rocking back and forth, or other body-stimulating movements*]. When they start knitting, no more stimming. This also works well with autism. Once they do something with both sides of brain, it works well.

My hope is that people at least try this. When they see how it works, maybe then it will be more widely available.

―――――――

There you have it: how knitting worked in a small but profound study, and that it can work for almost anyone.

By the way, I also asked Dr. Birmingham if the research team had tried crochet. He said no, based on the perception that it was a single-hand activity. I told him that I use both hands in crocheting, and he found this interesting. Maybe someone will do a similar study with crochet.

I've shared Dr. Birmingham's findings with everyone I've talked to about medKNITation. The science is fascinating, the potential for helping people is remarkable, and the bottom line is simple: stitchwork works.

Now that you know even more about how knitting can benefit us, let's medKNITate!

PART II
THE GUIDED MEDKNITATIONS

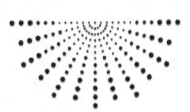

THE BASIC MEDKNITATION
"PATTERN"

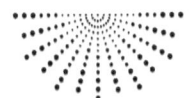

What makes medKNITation different from simply sitting down to knit or crochet? A series of easy-to-learn steps that turn stitchwork into a meditation that you can enjoy and benefit from every day. It's your very own knitting meditation!

Of course, before you can practice medKNITation, you'll need something to knit, or crochet, or stitch in some way. As I mentioned, medKNITation can be practiced with any form of stitching. Drawing on my own experience and that of hundreds of people I've led through medKNITation, I'll refer mostly to meditating with knitting and crochet.

WHAT PROJECT IS BEST FOR MEDKNITATION?

Many knitters and crocheters love to challenge themselves with new patterns and techniques. That results in focus and a learning, figuring-it-out state of mind, rather than a meditative, letting-your-mind-relax state. For that reason, the best type of project for medKNITation is the simplest. Scarves, shawls, dishcloths, granny squares, blankets, the part of sweaters that require many rows of stockinette—any project with simple, repeated stitches that you know well is perfect for medKNITation. (This used to be called "mindless" knitting, but I like to call it "meditative" knitting.)

Because knitting is one of my favorite forms of meditation, most of my projects are meditative. I've made a lot of scarves, shawls, thousands of Kindness Hearts, and anything I can do on repeat without having to look at a pattern or do much, if any, counting. It's good to have at least one medKNITative project on hand, if not a few, so you don't get tired of looking at the same yarn. The most important part is simplicity. Anything you can do that isn't complicated will work for medKNITation.

At the beginning of each of the guided medKNITations in this book, you'll see the suggestion to begin the Basic medKNITation, the steps that form the foundation for turning stitching into a meditation. Just as traditional forms of meditation have certain methods of sitting and breathing that help people ease into the mindset of their practice, medKNITation's steps set it apart from the kind of knitting we do for enjoyment. These steps are **Centering, Grounding, Awareness, Intention, Engaging,** and **Noticing.**

Though that may seem like a lot, the whole process takes only a moment or two, and each part is calming and enjoyable. (You can, of course, extend any part you like.) After doing this process a few times, you'll have it down like a pro!

Let's take a deeper look at each step and the how and why to do them. As you remember, that can increase the benefits you feel during the practice.

CENTERING

I once had a boss who, on very busy days, used to say, "I've lost my center!" I wasn't sure what he meant until I was able to find my own center through meditation practices—and how I lost that centered feeling on busy days, when I felt overwhelmed. Becoming centered means settling your body and mind so you can bring your awareness, or focus, to whatever you're about to do. In this case, it would be knitting, and that focus and activity become your meditation.

The first way to get centered is with the physical action of finding your seat. Our minds and bodies are not independent of each other; they are inter-dependent, working together, affected by each other. For example, if you feel physically unwell, your mind will likely be in some distress. If you're upset, or angry, you'll feel that somewhere in your body, like an upset stomach or a headache. (My husband used to think he was just prone to migraines until he switched from a high-stress job to one he felt truly happy in, and his twice-monthly migraine attacks became twice a year, if that.) In meditation, "finding your seat" means sitting in a way that will be comfortable, distraction-free, and that supports your body so your mind will also be comfortable and can ease into meditation.

To find your seat for meditation, start with a chair that allows you to sit upright, rather than curved and collapsed, the way we might sit in a recliner or couch. If you're sitting on that kind of soft area, try propping your back upright with some pillows. Sitting with a lengthened spine creates more space for your breathing, along with better ergonomics for more years of pain-free stitching. Try this experiment: Let yourself slump over, back curved, and take a deep breath. That probably wasn't the deepest, most satisfying breath you've ever taken. Now, imagine a beautiful strand of yarn extending from the base of your spine all the way up to the top of your head, so you're sitting tall with a gently lengthened spine, without stiffness or strain. Now take a deep breath. See how much deeper that breath is, and how much more air you gave your lovely lungs? Your whole body really appreciated that! I bet your mind did, too.

Let your shoulders be at a comfortable mid-point, not too far forward or back. Your jaw is level with the floor. Feeling comfortable and supported allows your body and mind to become settled. This helps you to create space and intention for the practice.

Your posture doesn't have to be perfectly straight, and if you have scoliosis, arthritis, osteoporosis, or any other condition that affects your spine and back, just sit in the way that's most comfortable for you. The first, and maybe only, rule of medKNITation: Work with what works for you! Always be compassionate with and kind to your wonderful, amazing body.

Don't Be a Shrimp

There are times when I've become so relaxed and focused on my stitching that I realize I'm almost completely curved over! This is fine posture for shrimp, but not for people. If it works for your body, make a practice of lifting your chest and bringing your arms out to your sides every few rows or ten minutes, whichever comes first. As with any movement, only do what feels good, never what causes any pain. Additionally, we tend to curve over to look at our work while we knit. Try bringing your project toward your face so you can keep your neck lengthened upward, chin level with the floor. If your project is heavy—love that blanket you're making!—put a pillow or two, or some folded towels, in your lap to bring it up higher.

GROUNDING

Being grounded often comes along with the idea of becoming centered. What does it mean to "get grounded"? My definition is feeling the connection between body and mind, and the best way I know to do that is through breathing practices.

As I wrote in my book *Yoga Mind: Journey Beyond the Physical*, my teachers taught me that the breath is the bridge between the body and the mind. I've learned many breathing practices in decades of studying Yoga and meditation. Part of what makes some of these practices a good form of meditation in themselves is the attention they require to do them properly. When I need to get grounded quickly, my favorite breathing practice is very simple: take three deep breaths, inhaling through the nose, exhaling through the nose. The exhalation is slow and intentional.

Why only three breaths in this exercise? When I lead the three grounding breaths in medKNITation, I encourage people to inhale and exhale to comfortable levels, but these breaths are deeper than our normal breathing, and we don't want to become breathless from inhaling too much or exhaling too far. Taking three comfortable breaths is just right. Here's a way to find that "just right" level of breathing: Think of something that makes you sigh with contentment—a finished project you love, an excellent meal, a relaxing moment in your garden, inhaling the scent of flowers—and make that sigh of contentment. That's the level of deep breath we're aiming for!

The three grounding breaths practice begins and ends with your own natural breathing pattern. The miracle of breathing is that our bodies do it automatically, without us having to think about it, but we can also use our minds to consciously change the way we breathe, taking a deeper breath, or breathing more slowly. How cool is that?

Knowing that we can consciously change our breathing is not only cool, it's important. When we're feeling anxious or fearful, our breathing becomes quick, shallow, and focused in the upper chest. This is part of the "fight or flight" or stress response, a system designed to help us prepare to do battle or run away. Most of the time, we don't need to do either; we're reacting to modern stresses where we don't actually have to escape or get ready to rumble.

Deep breaths are part of the parasympathetic nervous system, or "peace" response. You can bring on this peace response by taking a few deep breaths, which tell the body and the mind that everything is okay. Even if you're not stressed, taking a few deep breaths is calming and beneficial. Bring that healthy oxygen to your beautiful body and mind!

When we're not trying to alter the breath, our bodies, in their wisdom, know exactly how to breathe. Here's something you can try right now: Without altering your breath, put one hand on your chest and the other on your belly.

See if you feel any subtle movements that show you how you're breathing right now. Do you feel movement in your chest, your collarbones? The sides of your ribs? Your belly? There are no right or wrong answers. Your breathing may be very relaxed, so the movements might be too subtle to feel. Take one deep breath, let it out slowly, and see where you feel it. Let your body resume its natural breathing and see where you feel that.

When you're breathing naturally, meaning, you're not consciously altering the breath, your body is doing what it knows how to do. Your mind can simply observe that, which is a form of meditation in itself. Here's a bonus: by doing this exercise, you've just trained yourself in what it means to bring awareness to an action or a part of your body. You're meditating already!

Each medKNITation begins with three grounding breaths. This is a way of setting the intention to meditate, no matter where you are. I've done this on subways, in packed classrooms, and in hospital waiting rooms, and it really does give a sense of creating your own personal space for meditation.

Here's how to do the three grounding breaths exercise: Once you've found your comfortable seat and lengthened your spine, bring your awareness to your natural breathing pattern. Without altering your breathing, notice the inhalations and the exhalations. See if each inhalation flows into the exhalation, or if there's a space between the in-breath and the out-breath. There is no "right" or "wrong." Just notice, without judgment. Remember, noticing your breathing in this way is a form of meditation in itself. This is helpful if you're in a situation where you can't knit at the moment.

The three grounding breaths will be deeper than your normal breaths, but not so deep that you feel strain on the inhalation or that you're depleted when you exhale. Remember that sigh of contentment? That level of inhalation and exhalation should leave you feeling calm and good. The length and depth of each person's breath will be different and unique to them. As long as you feel comfortable, without strain or feeling breathless, you're breathing like a meditating pro.

For the three grounding breaths:

- inhale through your nose... exhale through your mouth.
- inhale through nose... exhale through mouth.
- inhale... and exhale.

Let your body return to its natural breathing pattern, breathing the way it wants to.

Just as we each have our own unique rhythm of making stitches, we each have our own pattern of breathing, and that changes as we go through the day. You've just used your mind to influence how you breathe with the three grounding breaths; when you're done, let your body resume the way it wants to breathe in this moment. Observe your breathing. Notice, without judging or changing the breathing pattern. Let your awareness rest gently on your body's own natural pattern of breathing for a few breaths.

AWARENESS

Becoming centered and getting grounded incorporates awareness through bringing your attention to your breathing and sensations in your body. Awareness is an important practice; as our minds become more distracted by digital devices, we may become more disconnected from our bodies. People sit for hours scrolling social media and playing video games, ignoring hunger pangs, aches from lack of movement, and desperate SOS signals from their bladders. Are we makers, whose mantra is "Just one more row," much different?

When I taught Yoga classes, students arrived frazzled from work and riding the crowded rush hour subway. After the class, they would tell me they didn't even know how stressed and tense they were until they brought their awareness to various parts of their bodies. Some of the students had become so disconnected from their bodies that, when I gave an instruction like, "Bring your left foot forward," they'd have to think for a minute before doing that. This step of the Basic medKNITation Pattern is a wonderful opportunity to get in touch with our amazing bodies while calming our brilliant, sometimes overloaded minds.

This practice is based on the Body Scan exercise by Jon Kabat-Zinn, founder of the Mindfulness-Based Stress Reduction program. MBSR uses techniques from ancient Yoga practices, and it's now a standard part of patient care in hospitals all over the United States and other parts of the world. In the Body Scan, your awareness travels through each part of your body, simply noticing, without judgment.

To do the Awareness practice, follow these steps at your own pace.

What If You Become Aware of Pain?

The practice of awareness is a way of noticing how you feel in each area of your body, but what if you have pain in areas of your body? Will you become even more aware of the pain?

Awareness is a way of noting, with compassion, not how you feel but what you feel. I have done this Awareness practice while dealing with sciatica that left me couch-bound, knee issues that had me in a leg brace, and two herniated discs in my neck that made my left shoulder feel like it was on fire. Rather than feeling more pain, awareness meant I was able to "pass through" that section of body-town just noticing: Okay, my back feels this way; my shoulder feels that way. Some parts feel better than others. We're not naming or judging anything. We're just being aware. If you don't want to experience awareness of that pain, simply acknowledge that part of your body ("Bringing awareness to my arm") and move on.

Another note about pain: My Yoga and meditation practice taught me that there is no "bad" part of our bodies. Students would say, "I have a bad knee," and I'd say, "You may have knee issues or a knee injury, but that's not a 'bad' knee. That's an awesome knee. It just needs a little extra attention and love." Our bodies don't want to feel pain—they're not doing this on purpose. The way I think about pain in my body is that something is happening. I give whatever is happening the attention it deserves, and if I can do something to alleviate the pain, I do it. If not, I just work with it.

No part of our bodies is "bad" or "wrong" or "broken." Our physical selves are glorious creations—whatever shape they're in, whatever's going on with them. Think of yourself as the steward of your body and treat it with loving compassion.

1. After establishing your comfortable seat and lengthening your spine, bring your awareness to your toes. You can wiggle them a little to lead your focus there. Then, move your awareness into your feet, feeling whatever they're on or in (shoes, those amazing stripey socks you made, fabulously furry unicorn slippers).

2. Move your awareness into your ankles, then your shins and calves, your knees; into the top of your thighs and the back of your thighs; your sitting bones, your hips.

3. Bring your awareness into your belly. Let your belly relax. We're encouraged in society to "suck it in." No need for that. As one of my wise teachers says, "Let the belly be the belly." Ah, freedom! Wrap your awareness around from your belly to your lower back.

4. Direct your awareness to your mid-back, and around to your ribs; up to your chest, and around to your upper back, including your shoulder blades.

5. Let your awareness go into your shoulders, and down into your upper arms, elbows, forearms, wrists, hands, and into each finger. You can flex your fingers gently here. It's worth paying a bit more attention to our fingers, hands, and wrists since these are our most valuable tools in stitching.

6. Lead your awareness up into your forearms, elbows, upper arms, and into the shoulders. From there, your awareness flows into your neck and throat; relax your throat muscles. Move your awareness into your jaw, ears, facial muscles, back of your head, brow, and the top of your head.

When you're finished moving your awareness throughout your body, return to noticing your natural breathing pattern.

Note: In a typical medKNITation session, the Awareness practice usually takes just a moment or two, but the practice can be used as a meditation by itself and take as long as you want. This is useful in situations where you can't knit at the moment.

INTENTION

This step is different from setting an intention, a direction or goal for your meditation, as you'll learn in the Intention medKNITation (page 86). In the Basic medKNITation, Intention means you're creating a space of time for yourself to meditate and dedicating your stitching during this time as a meditation.

When I began to knit and crochet as a meditation practice, I felt as though I was able to create a kind of personal, almost protective space around myself. Intention helps you create your own calming space. It's like the magic circle you may have drawn around yourself as a child. Knitting and crochet bring with it a sense of peace; this doesn't have to be a happy accident. It's empowering to know we can create this ourselves. Intention is a way of declaring that this knitting session is your meditation. I approach my daily meditative stitching time in this way, and the feeling is very different from the stitchwork I do when I'm watching TV.

The Intention step of medKNITation happens naturally when you do the previous and following steps.

ENGAGING

Meditation has a reputation for being a bit difficult. Our minds can take a while to settle and quiet down, and sometimes we give up before this happens—if it happens at all. Frustration can set in, and before we know it, we're saying, "I can't meditate!" When that happens, having a point of focus can really help. Your breathing can be a point of focus. You can focus on a mantra, or affirmation, as you repeat it in your mind. (I'll share examples of mantras to knit by in an upcoming chapter.) Some people need a more tangible point of focus, like yarn. This is why people say knitting and crochet are so meditative—your meditation anchor is right in your hands!

Engaging helps reinforce this focus. In medKNITation, Engaging refers to pausing for a moment to engage our senses, mostly those of touch, sight, and sometimes hearing. Traditional forms of meditation call for withdrawing the senses to lead to a more inward experience. Engagement is a different path to that experience.

You can do this part with the project you're working on, or with a ball or skein of yarn. After the previous steps, take a moment or two to engage your senses with your yarn. First, since your eyes may be closed from the calming initial steps of the medKNITation process, engage your tactile senses: touch your yarn with your fingertips. Hold it in your palms. Take a strand between your fingers and notice how the woven fiber feels. (Those with sight limitations will be familiar with engaging with yarn in this way.) You can engage your sense of hearing by noticing any sounds around you: birds outside, the gentle hum of appliances in your home. If the sounds are not pleasant—I had to listen to jackhammers outside our apartment for months—observe them, and then let them fade into the background by bringing your focus back to the yarn. Whatever you put your focus on is amplified.

Next, look at your yarn. Notice the colors. Your yarn may be one color, but there are other colors within that color, as well as parts in light and shadow. If you look closely, you may be able to see the smaller fibers that make up the strand. If you're meditating on a work in progress, look at your stitches; rows of orderly stitches and repeated patterns can calm the mind.

To engage another sense, you can even sniff the yarn. See what it smells like. Try not to label the scent "pleasant" or "unpleasant"; simply notice it. When working with wool, there may be a scent of lanolin.

As for engaging the sense of taste, I'm not suggesting that you taste your yarn, though that's completely up to you! Bringing a nice cup of tea to your medKNITation can be the way you engage your sense of taste, sipping slowly, noticing temperature and flavors.

NOTICING

Before the Age of Distraction, when screens began grabbing our attention as much as possible, I noticed more. I was aware of weather, the feeling of temperature and breezes, the quality and amount of sunlight at different times of day, and what comes with different seasons. I noticed smells and sounds, people—what they wore, how they moved through the world. I may have even been more attuned to the tiny facial expressions that tell more truth than someone saying, "I'm fine." I don't remember having "re-entry" moments, where I had to come back into the world and the present, because I wasn't as disengaged as I am after peering unblinkingly into my phone for half an hour, an hour, who knows? I could definitely become that absorbed in a book, but the information, and the way I took it in, felt far different to me. (Also, before phones and apps and social media, I read a lot more books than I used to. Note to self...) I used to notice more because I was able to focus.

Today, I have to make a concerted effort not to multitask, doing a few things simultaneously and mindlessly. I don't vilify social media. I get inspired when I see what people are making online, and we all need to know what's going on in the world. My husband loves to watch movies and shows, and while I don't love everything we watch, knitting gives me something to do while we sit together.

When I'm doing more than one thing at a time, my ability to focus, and to notice things, goes down—and not just while I'm multitasking. We've all seen people mesmerized by their phones walking through the streets, sometimes into peril. (A segment called "Brain Hacking" from news show *60 Minutes* explains how apps are purposely engineered to tap into the addictive centers of our brains, making us literally addicted to our phones.) I've tried not to become hypnotized by my phone because there's so much in the real world that I want to see: the cherry blossoms in our neighborhood, the rescue dog with the hand-knitted sweater, that great coffee bar around the corner—*life*. There's so much life around us, all waiting to be noticed.

One of the aspects of knitting and crochet that I love and am so grateful for is that they encourage, even demand, my attention. If I don't focus, I'll drop a stitch or forget a row count and have to unravel a lot of work. I've seen people become so adept at knitting that they can stitch without looking at their work while they watch TV or talk or even jog. I don't want to become this skilled! The main reason I knit is for the way stitching cultivates inner stillness and increases my ability to focus, which then increases my capacity for noticing. When I focus, I notice, and when I notice, I can truly appreciate life.

The interesting part of Noticing is that you don't have to do anything for it to happen. As with the other steps of medKNITation, Noticing is the result of the previous steps—Grounding, Awareness, and Engaging. As you brought your attention to each of those steps, you were Noticing. The reason Noticing is part of the medKNITation process is for you to become actively aware of the difference between how it feels to notice—to be aware of your breathing, instead of just knowing it's always there; to deeply observe your yarn, and to become fascinated in the way, as a child, you were fascinated by the tender yellow petals of a buttercup, or the tiny dots on the shiny red wings of a ladybug. Noticing the small details of your breathing and yarn means you'll notice more of what's around you, notice how someone you love is feeling without them having to say a word. In other words, knitting helps us notice life more.

Those are the steps leading up to medKNITation. Each step of this process takes only a moment or so, but I've found them to be important and wonderful parts of easing into a knitting meditation. They've helped me turn knitting, which I began as a way to relax and have fun, into a peaceful meditation.

Now that you know the process, you can practice it as a meditation itself, and as the beginning to the guided medKNITations on the following pages.

When You Don't Have Much Time
In a rush? You can still medKNITate. If you need to get to that calm place as soon as possible, shorten the Basic medKNITation steps to the three grounding breaths to start your meditation. With practice, the rest of the steps will naturally come along. You may find yourself automatically adjusting your posture, moving your awareness through your body, then letting it rest on your breath, and engaging your senses, all within the space of a moment. Even five minutes of medKNITation can make a difference in your day!

GUIDED MEDKNITATIONS

On the following pages, you'll find a series of guided medKNITations you can use to build on the basic medKNITation practice. These are the medKNITations I've done with in-person groups and online at Vogue Knitting Live. They were inspired by personal experiences, the experiences of group members, and our collective experience as people living in this time.

The materials you'll need will usually be the same: a meditative project and your knitting needles or crochet hook. For some of the meditations, you'll need only a ball or skein of yarn. There will be a note about whatever tools you'll need at the beginning of all the medKNITations.

Another tool you might want to consider is a medKNITation journal. I love journaling, and I have several notebooks and sketchbooks around for different journaling purposes. In your medKNITation journal, you can keep track of which medKNITations you've done and make notes about thoughts you have during or after your medKNITations. A medKNITation journal is also a good place to draw any ideas you have for projects—you'll be surprised at what comes to you in a meditative state!—and tape pieces of yarn from your meditative projects on the pages. Any kind of notebook will do, though I encourage people to get whatever kind of journal makes them smile, with pretty covers, dot grids, no lines, whatever you like!

To do these guided meditations, read through the steps first so you can familiarize yourself with the basic idea and theme, and then do the medKNITation. Following the steps exactly isn't necessary, nor is memorizing the wording; all you need is the general idea of each meditation. Just as you can tweak patterns to make a sweater or cowl work better for you, feel free to adapt any of these medKNITations, changing wording or other parts to make them fit you better. The Basic Pattern is the only one you may need to refer back to and practice at first. Once you have that down, the rest will flow easily.

And now, my friend, let's medKNITate together.

THE GUIDED MEDKNITATIONS

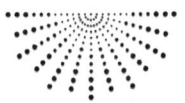

1

BREATHING MEDKNITATIONS 1 AND 2

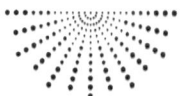

Yoga has been part of my life for many years. Though most people see Yoga as a form of exercise, I think of it as a moving meditation. I heard that suggestion at Integral Yoga Institute, the oldest Yoga studio in New York, where I took Yoga classes and trained as a teacher.

Through Integral Yoga, I was able to attend a Yoga conference where I heard a lecture by a teacher named Nischala Joy Devi. She took the stage with a radiant smile and a lovely combination of lavender and pink hair. In talking about meditation, specifically breathing meditation, she brought up a point made in many guided meditations: people are often instructed to inhale something beneficial, such as peace or calmness, and to exhale fear.

"By all means, breathe in that peace," Nischala said. "But exhaling fear? No, please—nobody should have to breathe in anyone else's fear!" The room full of serious Yogis suddenly burst out laughing. We'd never really questioned that meditation instruction, but the way Nischala said it, why would we ever encourage people to send out a whole lot of fear into the world to be breathed in by others?

Of course, the suggestion is a tool of visualization, which can be a helpful part of meditation. Directing someone to exhale fear can help them focus on the idea of fear leaving their mind and body. But, in the back of my own mind, I'd always wondered where my exhaled fear was going, and if it was being inhaled by someone else. *Yikes!*

Nischala, with all her wisdom, gave us a simple alternative: breathe in peace, and then exhale peace, love, or any other positive, beneficial energy. The idea is that if you visualize inhaling calm, any feelings of anxiety would be transformed, and you could exhale calm.

Then, Nischala led us in meditation so we could try it. *Breathe in peace... Exhale peace. Breathe in love... Exhale love. Breathe in calm... Exhale calm.* We did this for a few minutes, and when we opened our eyes, everyone in the room was smiling. No one had suffered any adverse effects by not "breathing out fear." In fact, we all agreed that just not using the word "fear" had resulted in a more positive experience, with our meditations being focused on peace, calm, and love.

This meditation combines breath awareness, stitching, and Nischala Joy Devi's suggestion to focus on positivity.

BREATHING MEDKNITATION 1: VISUALIZATION

Tools: your meditative project (anything super-simple, such as a garter stitch scarf), and your medKNITation journal.

Step 1: Follow the basic pattern for medKNITation (page 24).

Step 2: For a few moments, let your awareness rest gently on your natural breathing. You don't need to alter your breath at all. Take a deep breath when you feel like it, but otherwise, just observe your natural breathing pattern.

Step 3: Begin your stitching, going more slowly than your usual rhythm, as though you were showing someone how to make the stitches. Take a moment to notice each motion that goes into making a stitch, the feeling of the yarn as it moves through your fingers, the feelings and sensations in your fingers and hands.

Notice the spaces between the stitches. Think of them as breathing spaces.

Step 4: Bring your awareness back to your breathing. According to how you're feeling today, choose words that would be most beneficial for you to use in breathing visualization, such as the examples given before: *Peace. Love. Calm.*

Once you've chosen your visualization, without altering your breath, silently repeat that mantra to yourself. For example:

I inhale peace.

I exhale peace.

Visualize your word of choice as your favorite color, or a pleasing image that represents your meditative word, such as butterflies, a beautiful sky full of stars, or loving energy. Think of this image as you inhale, bringing this positive thought within, and exhale, sharing this positivity with the world. You can also direct this energy toward a specific person. You can shorten your mantra to *Inhale peace...exhale peace* if that goes better with your breathing and stitching.

Continue stitching for however long you like. When you're ready to finish this session, set your project in your lap and close your eyes. Do three grounding breaths to complete your meditation practice.

Breathing medKNITation 2: Breathing Pattern

Tools: your meditative project.

For this meditation, follow Steps 1 to 4 above, omitting the visualization and letting your awareness rest on your breathing. Allow the breath to be as it wants to be. Conclude the meditation with three grounding breaths.

2

MEET THIS DAY MEDKNITATION

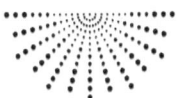

When I was a boy and I would see scary things in the news, my mother would say to me, "Look for the helpers. You will always find people who are helping."

— FRED ROGERS

Is today a "good" day, or a "bad" day? We're used to letting external circumstances decide that for us. A party or a fun celebration of some kind; a full day of work with lots of things going on; a medical procedure; or a farewell can all determine whether we think of a day as being "good" or "bad." So many things can affect how we think of a day, and that affects how we feel and respond throughout that day.

I remember one day in particular, years ago, when the sky was so blue and clear, the sun was shining so brightly, and the early fall weather was still warm, just right. I was doing Yoga that morning, which felt great. I was looking forward to a day of work that I liked doing. I thought, *This is a good day.* Minutes later, something happened that turned September 11, 2001, into one of the worst days imaginable. At first, the tragedy and shock were so immense, that's all anyone could focus on. We tried desperately to find something to hold onto.

And we did. We found the helpers. People helped in any way they could, coming together in response to the crisis, donating time, money, themselves. You didn't have to look far to find the helpers, from first responders at the scene to people making sandwiches for them.

The spiritual concept of equanimity is about finding and maintaining our composure, even in the face of difficulty—sometimes great difficulty. Facing challenges is part of life. We may lose our balance, but we can find our footing again, and then lend a hand to someone else. If we're the ones who need the hand, finding our equanimity can mean letting others help us.

In times of crisis, I've found that being useful helps. I acknowledge what I'm feeling, I accept the feelings, and then, I see if there's some way I can help. If I'm the one who needs help, I ask for it, and I let people help me. (Denial of needing help doesn't lead to anything good, but letting people help is a way to help others!) Being able to do something helpful is a way to channel strong emotions and bear them. I'm sure you've had experiences like that too. These are the experiences that bring us back to our own equanimity, and that connect us.

There are the large-scale world events that can affect our spiritual balance and our outlook on life, and then there are more personal times when life feels like a lot of heavy lifting. We wake up in the morning and wonder, *What kind of day is this going to be?* That question can be met with a sigh of resignation, or a deep breath to create a feeling of equanimity, of openness and curiosity, and maybe of gratitude for having a choice in how we meet each day.

As someone who has had periods of depression throughout my life, as well as going through the loss of friends, family, pets, and jobs—just like everyone else—I try not to let what's going on around me determine what kind of day I think this will be. Even in rough times, I can leave room for miracles. *Especially* in rough times. I can acknowledge that some things are definitely not going the way I'd want, and then I can see if there's a way to make it better. A call with a friend, some soothing knitting, a silly cat video. Even a little bit of balance can help.

Can we meet this day with equanimity, acknowledging the bad, appreciating the good? We can. On a beautiful, terrible day in

September, even through our tears, we saw the helpers. We found the good. And if we can't find the good, we can *be* the good in the day.

Meet This Day medKNITation

Tools: your meditative project.

This meditation is a good workout for the mind. We can let go of ideas of what this day "should" look like and set an intention to meet whatever comes with equanimity. When we get accustomed to meeting each day as it comes, and seeing what we can *bring* to the day, we're less likely to lose our balance as much, or for as long, before we get it back. This meditation also works if you're going through a rough time, or you're in a period of uncertainty. In those cases, we can meet each moment of the day.

Step 1: Follow the basic pattern for medKNITation (page 24).

Step 2: For a few moments, let your awareness rest gently on your breathing. In challenging times, your breathing pattern may vary, or even be shallow. That's okay. Let your breathing be where it wants to be in this moment.

Step 3: Start your knitting. Bring your awareness to your hands, your movements, the feel of the yarn moving between your fingers. Though you may have been making the motions that create stitches for so long that they're automatic, slow down a bit. Notice each motion that goes into making a stitch, as though you were showing a beginner how to do it.

Step 4: Think of the moments of the day as stitches, each one making up the fabric of this day. This day is made of many moments. You get to choose how to meet each moment.

Know that you are empowered to make this choice. You can feel your feelings, and you can find your equilibrium, your balance, your equanimity. Your true self. You can honor your feelings, create space for them, and know that they will change.

Set an intention to meet this day, and each moment in it, with acceptance.

Know that you can meet each moment with a sense of balance. You'll be able to take whatever is the next right action in that moment. Through giving yourself this time, you're connecting with your intuition. You will be guided as to what to do, even if that means not taking an action.

Say aloud or silently, "I meet each stitch of this day with acceptance and equanimity."

Continue stitching for however long you want. When you're ready to finish the meditation, set your project in your lap, close your eyes, and bring your awareness to your breathing. Do three grounding breaths, those comfortably deep inhalations and relaxing exhalations, to complete your meditation.

3
PATIENCE MEDKNITATION

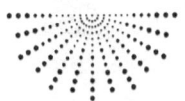

When I think about patience, I think about being on hold with the utility company that overcharged me, or the insurance company that didn't cover an approved medical test, and having to listen to terrible hold music that will stay in my head for the rest of the day. My patience really gets tested when I try to get past artificial intelligence mimicking a human so I can speak with an actual human. There's also the long supermarket line, the line at the post office, the waiting room at the doctor's office. Recently, I got home with the takeout food my husband and I were looking forward to having for dinner (book deadlines sometimes require the author not cooking, a perk of the work) and found that our bag was missing three parts of our order. I had to go back to get them, and try to be patient with the people at the restaurant who forgot to pack our food.

Our parents and grandparents were probably more patient than we are today, simply because they were used to waiting for things. Things took the time they took. In our time, we've been trained to expect immediate responses to our emails and texts, and people expect immediate responses from us. We used to wait, sometimes with excited impatience, for our favorite TV shows every week; now, if an entire season of a show can't be binge-watched in a weekend, we can't even deal. We can order something in a single click, sometimes for same-day delivery, faster than we can think about whether we really want or need it.

Knitting is the opposite of today's one-click culture. Knitting takes time. Some projects take months, even years. You make good headway on a project and then find a mistake, or see that the fit isn't quite right, and have to unravel most or even all of what you've done. Knitting requires patience.

The great news is that knitting also cultivates patience. Regarding the debate about "process" versus "project" knitters—those who knit for the knitting and those who knit to create something unique—author Melanie Falick told me, "We're *all* process knitters. Nobody knits because it's a fast, efficient way to get a sweater." There are many elements of the slow, steady knitting process that appeal to people. Working with your hands is a wonderful antidote to so much in our lives being automated and impersonal. You can create something yourself from raw materials, and something that lasts. Knitting is a skill often passed down from beloved family members, a worldwide family tradition. I love knitting for all these reasons, but one of the most important reasons is that knitting requires, teaches, and strengthens our power of patience.

We don't often think of patience as being powerful because we're focused on having to endure something, often grudgingly. When I get to enjoy the good feeling that comes with treating someone with respect and kindness, or when I don't lose my temper or my serenity, I see patience as one of my superpowers. It can be one of yours, too, and knitting helps to strengthen that superpower.

I have a shawl made of soft fingering yarn that goes from black to white to pink. (The yarn reminds me of my dear cat Ethel's black and white fur and her little pink nose.) I've been knitting this shawl for the past two years—not consistently, because I have a few projects going on at the same time, including non-knitting projects, like this book! I never mind how long it takes me to knit this shawl, though, because when I work on it, I get to dwell in a patient state where time feels slower. This is the kind of patience that's enjoyable.

The patience cultivated by knitting carries over into my non-knitting life. I notice that, on long lines, I'm relatively calm while others are muttering curses, even becoming rude with cashiers and postal employees. If somebody forgets part of my food order, I remember that they're human, like me, and just made a mistake, like I've made many, many times before.

Sometimes, I'll make a mistake in the middle of a sweater and have to unravel it so it can get corrected. If I lost my mind every time I made a knitting mistake, I might have written a book about gardening or Japanese calligraphy—neither of which I have the patience to do. Knitting cultivates patience. In this fast-paced time, knitting is a series of deep breaths.

I fully admit that I still get impatient with AI, yelling *"Representative! Agent! I want to speak to a real live person!"* into the phone. Once I connect with another human being, though, I can be patient, remembering all the calm times I've unraveled my work and knit it again without becoming unraveled myself.

PATIENCE medKNITation

Tools: any knitting project, simple or complicated, and your Yoga Mind journal (optional).

Patience is one of the many benefits that comes with knitting. Whenever we knit, we can meditate on the slow, steady rhythm, the row-by-row progress, and even the need to undo work to fix a mistake. Knitting cultivates patience that carries over into our daily lives, giving us the ability to simply smile as we let the other driver pass by, to breathe deeply while waiting on a long line. (I always bring a small knitting project with me for just that occasion. I guarantee you, I'm not only the most patient but the happiest person on the line. Have your knitting nearby if you expect to be on eternal hold on the phone, too. The hours will pass by like minutes.)

Stressful circumstances, such as hospital visits or medical tests, require a different kind of patience. In those situations, you have to patiently maintain your spiritual and emotional balance while waiting for news or results. Usually, the simpler the knitting project, the better it is for meditation, but if you're dealing with stressful circumstances, a complex project that requires counting and even referring to a pattern is better. That type of project requires a lot of focus, which provides a welcome distraction. In tense times that test your patience, bring on your intarsia, your steeking, your pattern with complex diagrams. They may not be the most meditative projects, and that may be exactly what you need.

Step 1: Follow the basic pattern for medKNITation (page 24).

Step 2: Breathing happens within your body, but it can affect your mind; likewise, your state of mind affects your breathing. The three grounding breaths are very important here. Take your time with them.

Step 3: Begin working on your project, bringing your awareness to your stitching. Engage your senses, paying attention to the colors of your yarn, the feel of the fibers as they slip through your fingers. Watch closely as you make your stitches. Observe what your fingers and hands are doing and how those movements feel.

For this meditation, you don't have to slow down. Knit or crochet at your usual rhythm. Follow your stitching rhythm with your eyes, and with your mind. Let the repetition soothe you.

Step 4: Consult your pattern as you need to. Write down rows. Do whatever calculations you need to do. Let yourself become completely absorbed in each part of what you're doing: knitting, reading the pattern, counting.

Continue stitching for however long you want. When you're ready to finish, set your project in your lap. Close your eyes. Bring your awareness to your breathing. Do three deep, comfortable grounding breaths to complete your practice.

4

COMPASSION MEDKNITATION

"Before you pick up your needles," my friend Alice said, an index finger announcing that I should pay extra attention to her words, "write out the pattern instructions."

"But they're already written out." I showed her the pattern I'd chosen for a moebius scarf. "Isn't that what a pattern is, instructions that are written out?" Beginners are funny; they always think they can find the shortcut that the person with years of experience, whom they're asking for lessons, has somehow missed.

Alice kindly overlooked my newbie know-it-all attitude. "Yes, the instructions are all right there in the pattern. But sometimes there's a mistake. And look at all the abbreviations. Do you know what they mean?" I only had to glance at the pattern to see the shorthand language of knitters: *kfb, ws, ssk, rep * to *.* I shook my head. "Well," Alice said, "you might have a smoother experience if you looked those up first. And who's to say there isn't something else you could work out before you're in the middle of a row?"

My friend's suggestion to write out patterns before I pick up my needles or hook has never been a waste of time. This can also be applied to explaining ideas, thoughts, and subjects of meditation. So, before we go further, I'll write out a few things.

As defined by the Oxford Languages dictionary:

Pity is the feeling of sorrow and compassion caused by the suffering and misfortune of others.

Sympathy is feeling pity and sorrow for someone's misfortune.

Compassion is sympathetic pity and concern for the suffering or misfortunes of others.

To a non-knitter, there's very little difference between a shawl, a scarf, a ruana, and a wrap. To those of us who stitch, we see the subtle differences instantly. In looking at the definitions of the words, there doesn't seem to be much difference between them. (I excluded empathy because it's defined as the ability to understand and share the feelings of another and doesn't necessarily involve pity or sympathy.) Compassion, though, has always stood out to me as being different than pity and sympathy. Maybe because part of the word is *passion*, which implies that the verve to do something more than merely feel sorry for someone or about something is built in.

Sympathy and pity have their place in our lives. There are times when we have to take a deep breath and realize that the only thing we can do for someone, or about a situation, is bear witness. This isn't an inaction, a sort of emotional consolation prize; it's a gift.

Then there are the times when we can feel compassion, which creates a connection. I'm reminded of my very first knitting teacher, Susan, showing me how to bind two pieces of yarn with a little spit and friction: so primal, and so effective. Compassion starts with connection, and then, with a little effort—a little spit and friction—we take action.

Chef José Andres couldn't stop natural disasters or wars, but he could feed people. His compassion for others was so great that he assembled teams of volunteers and went into dangerous parts of the world to give people in need the simple, profound comfort of a hot meal. The beginning of the organization known as World Central Kitchen, which has fed tens of thousands of people affected by natural disasters, political unrest, and a pandemic, began with compassion. Another example is Austin Rivers, who put his knitting skills to work to make hats, scarves, and gloves for homeless LGBTQ+ teenagers in New York and Chicago. Soon he launched Knit the Rainbow, an organization whose volunteers have made and given out thousands of garments to keep people warm in places where the winters are cold. While I'm meditatively slow at making garments, I asked Austin if Knit the Rainbow could use some Kindness Hearts to attach to the garments. "Sure," he wrote back, "Can you make about 800?" (I did, within four weeks, and those hand cramps were among the best feelings I've ever had.) There are so many stories like these, so many people who have felt compassion and taken action.

A person can look at a situation where help is needed and say, *Oh well, what can I do?* Another person can look at the same situation and think, *Hmm, what can I do...* People who make things are among the most creatively resourceful people I've ever met. Add to that the altruism that runs through the fiber community like a thread of gold, and you have compassion with agency, creating positive changes that can change lives.

What can you do?

COMPASSION MEDKNITATION

Tools: your meditative project and your medKNITation journal.

This meditation is about cultivating compassion—the willingness to be vulnerable and feel for others, along with the understanding that there may be some way to help.

Step 1: Follow the basic pattern for medKNITation (page 24).
Step 2: For a few moments, let your awareness rest gently on your natural breathing. Notice how each inhalation leads into each exhalation and back into each inhalation, like the loops we weave in knitting and crochet. Each breath is connected.
Step 3: Bring your awareness to your stitching, going slowly.

Notice the feeling of the yarn as it moves through your fingers. Notice how each loop is connected, as though holding hands. Think about how we are all connected.

Step 3: Bring to mind the times that someone has changed your day with kind words and a smile. Think of the power of these simple actions. Know that you have the power to create the same kind of positive change.

As your inhalation connects with your exhalation, as each stitch you knit connects with the one before and the one to come, know that you can make a difference. You're a maker, and you can make positive change. All we have to do is be willing to open our hearts to others.

Continue stitching for however long you like. When you're ready to finish, set your project in your lap. Close your eyes and bring your awareness to your breathing. Do three grounding breaths to complete your meditation. Write down any thoughts or ideas you had during your meditation in your journal.

5

EMOTIONAL STASH
MEDKNITATION

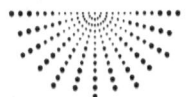

Every now and then, usually when yarn starts spilling out past a dedicated yarn bag, closet, or room, knitters do an inventory of our yarn stash. We look through all our skeins, hanks, balls, and leftovers and see what we want to keep and what we're ready to release. We do a little clearing (some of us, anyway), and the yarn collection feels more orderly. Maybe we even finish some of those works in progress!

Just as I do the occasional yarn stash inventory, I like to do an Emotional Stash Inventory. An inventory is about looking at what I have and assessing its value. When I do this medKNITation, I look at my habits and feelings, the way I think about myself, my work, my relationships to the various parts of my life. I consider what's working, what feels right, what's healthy and beneficial, and what I want to keep doing. Then I look at the things I'm not sure about. Can I change this for the better, make something new out of it, like unraveling a sweater that isn't working and repurposing the yarn? I also look at the things that aren't working, that don't feel good, or that have come to an end and that I need to release so I can move on. I try to be as objective as I can; this isn't about being "perfect."

Here's an example of how this meditation can work. For as long as I can remember, I've had a fear of financial insecurity. The roots of this fear were born in fact: My mother and I didn't have very much money when I was growing up. Sometimes Mom, who worked very hard, had to choose between paying a bill or buying food. She always made sure we ate, but we didn't always have a working phone. The fear of not having enough money remained with me, whether I had a steady job that paid well, or I was in between gigs. I've stayed in jobs that weren't healthy long after I should've said goodbye because I was afraid of not having enough money. Interestingly, it was only after some of these unhealthy working relationships ended that I'd go on to write a book or find other, better work. That fear of not having enough didn't become a fact.

I'd love to say that I medKNITated the fear of financial insecurity away in one cowl, but this isn't one of those manifestation tricks where you repeat a mantra for thirty days and you're suddenly rich. I had to be more present, realizing that my circumstances today are not what they were when I was a child. I had to sort through my feelings, the same way I go through my yarn stash. When I found this habitual feeling and recognized that it wasn't only not working, but working against me, I had to do something different.

For me, getting calm is the first step. Decisions made in fear aren't usually our wisest moves. Knitting is a great way to get calm. When I do that, I feel grounded and centered, I can start seeing options, and fresh, optimistic ideas come to me.

I've used the meditative time of knitting to address feelings I might not want to deal with, letting them tell me, in that quiet, calm space, why they've been sticking around; it's usually because I need to take an action. Of course, the similarity of the yarn stash inventory and the emotional stash inventory splits there. Letting go of yarn you don't like is a lot easier than to "just let go" of emotions and feelings we've had for years, sometimes all our lives. Yet even if we can't let go entirely, we may be able to find a way to make peace with things. All we need is the willingness to get calm, look at the situation as objectively as we can—"Is this working for me?"—and consider our options for what to do with it. (If it's a big issue, one of those options is talking to a therapist, social worker, member of your religious or spiritual group, or a friend or family member you can trust, and who will listen to you calmly and help you to feel better.)

Making the emotional stash list can take place over one medKNITation or several. I write down what I've found, and then—this is the really good part—instead of putting all my energy toward letting go of the things I don't like about my feelings, I focus my energy on the things I *do* like. You can focus on what's working for you and what brings good to your life and the world around you. By bringing your powerful energy to those positive parts, you naturally diminish the negative parts, like in the Native American fable about the two wolves, the wolf of positive energy and the wolf of negative energy. Which wolf is stronger? The one you feed.

During a yarn stash inventory, you may come up with ideas for projects for the yarn you love. In this meditation, you'll be inspired by focusing on your positive attributes. Who knows what good you can create when you bring your radiant energy to the best parts of yourself?

EMOTIONAL STASH MEDKNITATION

Tools: Your meditative project, and your medKNITation journal to record any thoughts or insights you have.

Step 1: Follow the basic pattern for medKNITation (page 24).

Step 2: Begin stitching, bringing your awareness to your hands, your tools, and your yarn. Though you may have been making stitches for so long that your movements are automatic, slow down a bit. Notice each motion that goes into making a stitch. Notice the feeling of the yarn as it moves through your fingers. Notice the feelings and sensations in your fingers and hands. Follow the yarn as it loops through previous loops, a single strand creating woven mesh.

Step 3: Allow any thoughts, feelings, or habits you've been noticing lately come to your conscious mind. This may be a mix of emotions and/or habits, in the same way you have different types of yarn in your stash.

Make an agreement with yourself: For now, you're noticing these emotions, thoughts, and habits without judgement, like when you've observed your breathing. During this meditation practice, you're observing, labeling nothing "good" or "bad."

Notice which habits, thoughts, and emotions have been helpful and supportive to you. Write them down in your journal.

Step 4: Next, think of habits, thoughts, and emotions that have not been so helpful or beneficial. Maybe they were useful at various times in your life, but, like tools that have become rusty, bent, or broken, they're no longer working. Again, we're not calling them "good" or "bad," just "helpful" or "not useful." Pause in your stitching to write these down.

Bring your awareness back to your positive habits, thoughts, and emotions. Set an intention to bring more energy to those positive attributes and actions. Think of all the good that can come from feeding these positive aspects of your life with your powerful energy!

Continue stitching for however long you want. Be open to fresh ideas. When you're ready to finish, set your project in your lap. Close your eyes and bring your awareness to your breathing. Do three grounding breaths to complete your meditation.

6

INVITATION TO JOY
MEDKNITATION

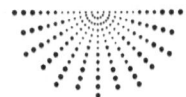

A few years ago, I came across a TED Talk by Ingrid Fetell Lee, an artist who spent years studying an interesting subject: joy.

During a critique of Ingrid's artwork, her teachers and peers said Ingrid's work inspired feelings of joy. That sounded wonderful, but she wondered what that meant. What is joy? Is it like happiness, or different? Is it more intense, but more fleeting? Ingrid began researching the elements of joy. She studied art, architecture, culture. She asked people what brought them joy. The answers provided a consistent picture of the elements that create a joyful feeling: things that are soft, round, and colorful.

Sound familiar? That's what we see in a yarn shop.

Children have soft toys, brightly colored crayons, confetti, and other joyful items. Their daily tools, like dishes and toothbrushes, have those joy-inducing elements built in. When we become adults, we enter a world of sharp angles and dull colors. No wonder we're so hungry for those intense bursts of happiness!

Joy usually comes as an unplanned surprise. We're delighted by something we didn't expect, even if we're hoping the trip goes well or the event we planned is everything we wanted it to be. But joy doesn't have to be random. When you're hungry for food, you don't wait or hope for dinner to "happen." You make it, or you ask someone to bring you a delivery of freshly-made pizza or savory Chinese food. It's the same with joy—we don't have to wait for it. We can invite more joy into our lives.

In recent years, the word "joy" was applied to the act of clearing out one's home. (To clear up a common misconception, Marie Kondo was actually referring to keeping the possessions that make you feel joy, not that purging everything in your life would make you more joyful.) Is joy the same as happiness? Spiritual and religious paths assert that happiness isn't about material possessions—how long does that new yarn high last anyway? Not long, judging from my continually renewing stash—but more about a feeling of lasting, overall contentment, regardless of circumstances, that comes with balance, acceptance, and being comfortable with yourself.

Less is said about joy, though. I could cite the dictionary here, but I'd rather ask you: What makes you joyful? What brings you that fizzy elation, the feeling of your spirit soaring? What makes you giggle and feel giddy? The definition of joy can be unique to each person. We can have our own bouquet of whatever brings us joy in life.

The feeling of joy can happen spontaneously, and we can also invite more of it into our lives. Life is very busy, and we're constantly doing, having very little time to *be*. Our sense of value has shifted to how much we can pack into the day and checking tasks off an endless to-do list. That's satisfying, but let's make space for some joy, please!

This medKNITation looks at inviting joy, intentionally, into life through something we know gives us that instantly fizzy feeling: smooshing colorful, soft, fuzzy balls of yarn. That may sound silly, but what's wrong with that? Never underestimate the power of our tactile senses to evoke emotions and bring us into the present moment—which can become an experience of joy.

INVITATION TO JOY MEDKNITATION

Tools: a new ball, skein, or hank of yarn, or unused yarn you currently have on

hand, preferably in bright colors, and the needles or crochet hook that are
appropriate for the yarn.

Step 1: Follow the pattern for the Basic medKNITation (page 24).

Step 2: For a moment or two, linger on the Engaging step. If your eyes are closed, gently open them. While holding your yarn in your lap, take in the colors of your yarn; maybe there are several. If it's one color, see how the light affects the colors as you hold it.

Look closely at the fibers, noticing how they make up the strand.

Feel your yarn, first with your fingers, then on your cheek.

Are there varying textures in your yarn? Notice everything you can about this fiber.

Now, cast on twenty or so stitches for a swatch.

Step 3: As you begin stitching, invite joy into your consciousness by thinking of joy as a friend who would love to visit you more often. All you have to do is think about what brings you joy.

As you stitch, bring the ingredients of your joy into your consciousness. If you like, you can use one-word descriptions, like these examples: *Popcorn. Garden. Birthday. Yarn. Dogs. Bubbles. Beach.*

Here's an affirmation you can recite with each stitch, silently repeating to yourself:

I weave joy throughout my life.

When you're ready to complete this meditation, let your project rest in your lap, close your eyes, and finish with three grounding breaths. Write your experience and any thoughts that came to mind in your journal. And make a list of the things you can do to bring more joy into your life!

7

MAKE A DIFFERENCE
MEDKNITATION

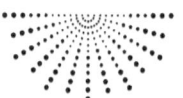

The Martian, the novel by Andy Weir and, later, the movie starring Matt Damon, is about an astronaut who becomes stranded alone on Mars. That would seem to be science fiction, but there's a deeper message. I'm not giving away any spoilers when I tell you the basic plot: Mark, who faces a slow, painful, lonely death if not rescued, reflects on his crew's audacious plan to save, as he refers to himself, "one dorky botanist": *...Every human being has a basic instinct to help each other out. It may not seem that way sometimes, but it's true.*

Mark acknowledges that there are people who don't care about others (using a more colorful term), but that they're vastly outnumbered by people who do. We do care, a lot. We want to help, even when we don't know how to help.

Knitters and crocheters usually find a way.

This desire to help and take action made knitters an important part of history. During World Wars I and II, the "Knit Your Bit" movement in the U.S. and the U.K. provided socks, sweaters, hats, and other garments for soldiers in action, all made by civilians when factories couldn't keep up with the need or get supplies. Everyone knitted for the cause—men, women, children, at home and at work. More recently, knitters have responded to disasters with handmade garments, and they've raised awareness for causes with craftivism, a form of activism using crochet, cross-stitch, and knitting.

In 2022, when the Russian army launched an unprovoked attack on Ukraine, my husband and I made donations to the charities racing to the scene with aid; wanting to do more, I crocheted blue and yellow flags of Ukraine, along with sunflowers, the national flower of Ukraine, and gave them out to anyone who wanted them, and for donations to organizations bringing aid to Ukraine. Still, at times, my fingers cramping from crocheting so many sunflowers, I wondered: *What good will this do?*

The answer came months later. My husband goes to a local Yoga studio, where one of the teachers is from Ukraine. When she taught a class with proceeds going to organizations helping Ukraine, my husband took some of the flags and sunflowers I'd made to give to everyone in the class. When I met the teacher, almost a year after the initial invasion, she greeted me with a hug and tears in her eyes. "Thank you," she said. "I can't tell you how much it helped to know that people here cared."

We care. We want to help each other out. It may not seem that way sometimes, but it's true. When we've done all we can to directly address a situation, a disaster, a catastrophe, we may still feel helplessness fraying us at the ends. That's when we sit down and create something that may one day show someone that the problem may not be solved, but we care.

When we make something from a place of caring, we can make a big difference.

MAKE A DIFFERENCE MEDKNITATION

Tools: your meditative project.

When faced with a situation that makes us want to do something, creative thinking is the antidote to despair or, worse, apathy. (Whatever you don't do, don't become apathetic! There's always a way to help, even by just caring.) Being of service is one of the greatest gifts we can give, and one of the greatest gifts we can receive. How to help can come to us in meditation.

My personal experience, and maybe yours, is that ideas don't come to me if I sit down and try to think of a solution. That's like saying all we have to do to get a good night's sleep is tell ourselves, "Okay, sleep." That doesn't work too well, does it? Good ideas have come to me when I'm washing dishes, or in the shower, or knitting, doing things that keep my motor skills moderately engaged and my mind free to receive inspiration and guidance. Knowing this can be useful the next time you want to do something to help.

Step 1: Follow the basic pattern for medKNITation (page 24).

Step 2: Take three grounding breaths, and then let your body breathe however it wants to. If you'd like, set an intention to be open to inspiration.

Step 3: Let your awareness rest on your natural breathing. Notice the rhythm of your inhalations and exhalations without changing them. Your body has its own breathing pattern, and your mind is just gently observing it now.

Bring your focus to your nose. Notice the feelings of the inhalations, cooler air entering your nostrils, then warmer air leaving in the exhalations.

Your mind may start to wander. Let it. Without actively trying to think of anything, whether the problem you'd like to do something about or a solution, let your mind drift. From time to time, you can gently steer your focus back to your breathing, and then, let it drift away again.

Some thoughts and ideas may come to you about the solution you're seeking. Let them. See what comes when you receive these thoughts and ideas.

When you're ready to conclude your meditation, bring your focus back to your breathing, feeling the inhalations and exhalations again. Take three grounding breaths, and, before you resume your day, pause for a moment of gratitude. Write down your thoughts in your medKNITation journal.

8

CLOSURE MEDKNITATION

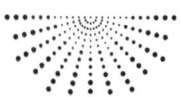

The fact that fiber arts like knitting and crochet, as well as quilting, sewing, and spinning, are meditative is no secret in the worldwide fiber community. In recent years, that has been the main reason many people have taken up these crafts. Scientists and researchers also heard about this and set about studying it, as Dr. Birmingham did with his patients in the eating disorder clinic. The word was out: Knitting, crochet, and other forms of stitchwork were forms of meditation.

Most traditional forms of meditation don't come with a big shopping component, though.

In the beginning, I pictured myself as a monogamous stitcher, working on one project at a time until it was finished. If you're a knitter or crocheter, I can almost hear you laughing, likely from a seat made of piles of yarn because you've run out of room for your stash. Within my first month of knitting, I succumbed to the lure of new yarn for more projects, or just new yarn for no particular project. I'd see a sample at a yarn shop, or get an email about yarn kits or a sale, and I'd think, *Well, I'll be done with my current project soon... I should get more yarn.*

And some more. And another kit. Because you can't have too much yarn? ...Can you?

At some point in my yarn accumulation, I learned a new term: UFO. Not the *X-Files*, Area 51, Unidentified Flying Objects version, but the Un-Finished Objects version. I'd start a project, work on it for a while, and then find some absolutely yummy new yarn and a fresh pattern for a garment that would surely Change My Life. That happened many times. I have no idea if the finished projects would change my life because I never finished them.

I read somewhere that the reason people buy so many books, even when they have stacks not yet finished or even begun, is because what they're really buying is a fantasy that they will one day have the time to read all these books. They have a vision that someday, they'll be curled up on a comfy chair, cup of tea and cat nearby, with all the time in the world to read.

Is it the same with yarn? Speaking for myself, a few things came together to form a mass of yarn and UFOs in my closet (and my bookcase, and under our coffee table, and in one of those large blue shopping bags). One was community. As a person who has worked at home alone for years, going to a yarn shop is an experience that releases many happy chemicals in my brain. Whenever I visited my favorite yarn shop, I'd be warmly greeted by old friends and make a few new ones, talk to live human beings, and feel the joy induced by all the colors and softness of many balls, hanks, and skeins of yarn. And you can't go to a yarn shop without buying yarn.

All of this added up to me being a very happy yarnaholic. What started out as a fun experiment became a habit. My husband began to look wary. "Maybe you should try finishing one project before starting another?" he asked as my project bags multiplied in the living room. "Great idea," I said, not mentioning the three hanks of yarn I'd just bought during a Yarn Crawl and the kit I'd ordered. (Those cats were out of the bag when I needed his help in winding the yarn. For the record, my husband always helps me wind yarn, without complaint, and whenever we see a yarn shop in our travels, he asks if I'd like to check it out. He is what is known as a wonderful Yarn Husband.)

Occasionally—usually after getting my credit card bill—I'd put together all my unfinished projects, which I'd reframed as works in progress (WIPs). What's the difference between a WIP and a UFO, after all? That reframing worked for a while, but there are only so many projects I can classify as being current. A work in progress is something that's progressing because I'm working on it now, or at least recently. But when a WIP hasn't been out of a project bag for months, sometimes years, it becomes a UFO, lost in a galaxy of project bags.

Twice a year, I do a yarn inventory. During one of those missions, I saw how many WIPs were really UFOs. I was surrounded by half-sweaters I'd forgotten I started, random sleeves, and partial pieces I couldn't even identify. I began to feel the opposite of the way knitting makes me feel. What I had was not a pile of WIPs or UFOs, but a lot of unfinished business.

The fiber arts provide many metaphors for life lessons. A UFO is not only an unfinished object, but unfinished business. We can have a lot of that in our lives. Projects begun to be completed "someday." Things we want to do, but don't. Endings we weren't prepared for—jobs, relationships, the loss of people we love—and haven't fully come to terms with so we can find closure and peace. That doesn't always come when we want it. We have to work on it, the same way we have to work on projects.

Unfinished business and the unresolved feelings that come with it aren't always about upsetting subjects. Just as closure can be healing for situations that are sad, it can also acknowledge experiences that have been wonderful and help us feel happiness and satisfaction more deeply. Either way, closure creates fertile ground for honoring an experience, and it allows us to process what we've learned and grow from it.

In a sense, this is what meditation is about: to be with something, learn from it, and prepare to move on to your next steps. One day you sit in meditation and it's all beautiful colors and feelings of peace. Next day, the supermarket list and an annoying song march through your mind ceaselessly. The day after that, it's something different. In meditation, you sit with whatever happens that time, learn from it, and move on.

With the unfinished business of our lives, sometimes it's not so easy to move on. We can do that when we get closure of some kind, but that's not always available. Maybe the chance to wrap things up neatly came and went. We may not want to revisit the experience that lacks closure because it could hurt us or others, or the person who could help give that closure isn't here anymore. What then?

Years ago, there was an organization I wanted to work with, and I managed to create an opportunity to collaborate. For a while, the work went well, but over time, the relationship became strained. One day, we arrived at the point where I said things had to change or I would have to leave. I didn't mean it as an ultimatum, but to show how far our original arrangement had strayed off course. The reply was brief and brusque: "Then go."

The swiftness of the end left me wishing for something that had been more mutual and peaceful. That wasn't likely to come from the other person. The unfinished business of coming to terms with this was on me.

This is where knowing that we have the ability to choose is such a valuable spiritual tool. We get to decide what deserves our precious energy and what doesn't. I haven't always known that I had the power to create my own sense of closure and move on, but I learned that we don't have to depend on other people or circumstances to grant closure. This is excellent news; the power to find our own way of saying, "This is complete, and I'm ready to move on" is within each of us.

In knitting and crochet projects, I felt free to stop in the middle of working and go on to the next project. Maybe I exercised that right a little too often, judging from the number of unfinished objects I have. In empowering spiritual terms, we can also exercise the right to choose when and how we create our own sense of closure. We choose when we can form a feeling of acceptance, and even peace, around an experience, in the same way that a tender oyster has the power to form a beautiful, luminous pearl around a painful grain of sand.

Sometimes it's easier for us to consider a concept like closure by using a metaphor, such as those unfinished objects we stitchers seem to accumulate. To do this meditation, pick one of those and have it in hand, along with the tools (needles or hook) you need to keep going with it, should you decide to do so.

Closure medKNITation

Tools: your meditative project.

Step 1: Follow the basic pattern for medKNITation (page 24).

Step 2: For a few moments, let your awareness rest on your natural breathing pattern. Notice how one breath moves naturally to the next, as one stitch leads to the next, and the next.

Step 3: As you look at the unfinished project in your hands, think of an event that you want to feel closure around. Just as you have the power to decide whether or not to continue this project, you have the power to decide that you're ready to accept the unfinished business and move on.

Your life energy is precious. You are empowered to decide what you grace with that divine energy.

Time is precious. As you feel your unfinished object, ask yourself if you want to dedicate the time and energy it will take to finish it. The decision to continue and finish it, or to decide you'd like to direct your energy and time to other things, is yours.

Understand that closure is yours to create, a decision you make to direct your energy to areas of your life that you would prefer to help grow and thrive.

Say aloud, "I honor the experiences I've had with this, and I'm ready to move on."

Step 4: Now you can begin taking your next steps. You can make a few stitches in your project, progressing forward, or unravel the project so the yarn can be repurposed. Either way, you have created your closure, and you're moving forward.

Continue stitching or unraveling for however long you like. When you're ready to finish the meditation, close your eyes, bring your awareness to your breathing, and do three grounding breaths to complete your practice.

9

HIGHER CONSCIOUSNESS CROCHET MEDKNITATION

This is a crochet-specific meditation primarily because crochet allows you to take twists and turns and create shapes within a project, where knitting is more about orderly rows.

Now, this could take us into the occasional divide between knitting and crochet. Or, as people say, "Do you knit *or* crochet?" When I was a novice, brand-spankin' new to the world of fiber arts, I wondered why people had to choose between the two.

There are people who are just as happy crocheting as they are knitting and who make a regular practice of both, depending on their mood and the project. Sometimes the people who do both have a favorite, in the same way people who draw have a favorite medium— watercolor over markers, colored pencils over ink. But there are people who prefer to knit *or* crochet. They learned one and not the other, or they fell in love with one and lived happily ever after. I thought I would be that way with knitting too. But... I liked the look of the jabbing action of crochet.

My entry into the world of fiber arts was through knitting, chiefly because the friend who asked if I wanted to join her for classes was taking knitting lessons. This was, as you may remember, during a very stressful time for me. If my friend had said she was taking crochet lessons, I'd have said yes. I'd have said yes to cricket lessons, glass blowing lessons, bridge lessons, anything short of mixed martial arts training, and even then, if she'd promised dinner after, I'd probably have said yes.

So, I became a Knitter, making orderly row after orderly row. This was very meditative. Very relaxing. Very predictable, just one sweet stitch after the other. At a time when there seemed to be a fresh calamity every week, predictability was what I wanted.

Fast forward a few years. One night, while scrolling through movies available to watch, I found a documentary called *Yarn*. My husband was working late; supportive as he is of my knitting habit, I thought he might be equally supportive of me watching this without him, and I eagerly pressed play.

The documentary was not about yarn per se, but about artists expressing their creativity with fiber, specifically through crochet. This wasn't what I expected—and it was completely riveting. Not only were these women making art with fiber, which was a revelation in itself, but this was the first time I'd seen crochet in action, rather than just a still photo of a crochet project. The artists hooked quickly, with gusto: *jab jab jab!* Their hands and hooks were like hummingbirds, a blur of color and movement.

Did I blink at all throughout that documentary? I was thoroughly captivated by crochet. Something about it made me want to learn it immediately. At the time, I might not have been able to articulate the reason why, aside from the fascination of watching the motions and the creations. I understood more when I tried crochet a few days later.

I secured a hook—I already had plenty of yarn—and found a book called *Stitch N' Bitch Crochet: The Happy Hooker* by Debbie Stoller, who is also the author of several knitting books. Apparently, crochet had a wry sense of humor, so I loved it already. I sat down and followed the instructions for how to crochet, or tried to, at least. Like anything new, the first few times were slow and clunky. I felt like I was learning to knit again, but this time, without the dread of the dropped stitch. (Lose a stitch in knitting and you'd better catch it fast before it goes into a freefall ladder *alllll* the way down your project. Lose a stitch in crochet and it just hangs out patiently. *No worries*, it says. *I'll wait.*)

When I became a little more fluent in crochet, I discovered why making loops with a hook appealed to me: anxiety.

This may be just me, or it may be the reason some people gravitate to crochet more than knitting. I've had bouts of anxiety here and there all my life. In these times of people being more open about their feelings and mental health, I've found that I'm in very good company. When I'm anxious, I have nervous energy that needs to be expelled. I would go for a run if my knees hadn't informed me years ago that they were retiring from that form of exercise. When I saw those crochet artists in the documentary making those *jab jab jab!* motions, that spoke to some part of me. Some jumpy little part that wanted to jab my way to relaxation.

This might also be why crochet is used in schools and by craft-savvy parents to help children who have too much energy and too little focus. (Note: that's a personal theory, not one based on research, which has yet to be done on this worthwhile subject.) One of the most popular crafters in America is Jonah Larson, known online as Jonah's Hands. As Jonah and his mom Jennifer described on the *Today* Show, Jonah occasionally acted out in class at school. His mom suggested he learn to crochet, which he did at the age of five by watching YouTube videos. Jonah's teacher allowed him to bring his crochet to class after seeing how it helped him focus. The result? No more disciplinary problems. Jennifer Larson described crochet as "medicinal."

When I heard this story, as well as stories from legendary knitting teacher Cat Bordhi about the calming effects of knitting on the children and teenagers she taught in school, I couldn't help but think that crochet and knitting should be a regular part of learning for kids. If it can't be part of a curriculum, people like my dear friend Louis Boria start knitting and crochet clubs for kids after school.

Another interesting thing I found out about crochet is that it doesn't always need to follow an orderly pattern. Yes, knitting can create shapes too, within its language of neat rows. Crochet has the option of making neat rows too, but it's also willing to go completely free-form jazz at any point in a project. Make a wave? Sure! How about a really curly wave? *Awesome!*

Crochet's willingness to create twists and turns at will was something I experienced when using my scrap yarn pile to practice various crochet stitches, increases, and decreases. Making the stitches over and over, and then switching them up, sometimes mid-row, allowed my mind and hands to connect without ideas of "right" and "wrong" getting in the way. My mind might say, *You can't do that!* Crochet's response is, *Ooh, let's do that!* My consciousness floated as my hands created waves, curls, graceful octopus arms.

My practice swatch grew and grew into a meditation project. Whenever I felt anxiety creeping up on me and my thoughts began to ping-pong around my head, I'd reach for my Higher Consciousness Crochet Project. (I've also heard it called a Stash-ghan and a Scrumbling project.) Knowing that I had no pattern to follow and no rules to obey was freeing. My thoughts calmed with each random loop as I watched my hands jabbing away. If I didn't like the way part of it was going, I could rip it out without any feeling of loss or frustration. After all, you may like this collection of various types of yarn, stitches, and shapes enough to use it as a blanket or a wall hanging, but it's not a formal project. It's a meditation.

If you're a crocheter, you may already have a project that you add to from time to time, as I do. If you're a knitter who has never tried crochet, think of it this way: There's classical music and there's free-form jazz, there's thin-crust New York style pizza and deep-dish Chicago style, there's Ashtanga Yoga and Yin Yoga and Yoga for arthritis... Each one is great; it just depends on your mood. Maybe the idea of creating your own meditative art project will appeal to you enough to get a hook, check out Debbie Stoller's book or Jonah's videos on YouTube, and jab to your heart's and mind's content.

HIGHER CONSCIOUSNESS CROCHET MED**KNIT**ATION

Tools: a variety of crochet hooks and yarn. This is a great project for all those little balls of extra yarn that aren't enough for a whole project.

Like the crochet meditation project itself, there is no pattern for this meditation. The point is doing something that can help you strengthen your connection with your intuition by letting your mind wander with your hands. In terms of colors and types of yarn to use, go by feel, meaning a combination of emotional as well as physical feel. In addition to material from almost every project I've made, my Higher Consciousness Crochet Project includes yarn I used to make charity scarves, shawls I wear often, and my late biological father's chemo hat. There is a map of memories in this collection of meditative stitches.

Step 1: If you're feeling anxious, begin with some physical movement to release the excess energy. Try dancing or a few Yoga Sun Salutations.

Step 2: Find a comfortable seat and follow the pattern for the basic medKNITation (page 24).

Step 3: Begin to crochet. (You can, of course, do this meditation with knitting.) Cast on as many stitches as you want, making a chain, or make a circle. Use any stitches you like. Don't plan your stitches; let your mind be free to choose whichever ones you use.

Observe your movements. Follow your hands, your fingers. Bring your awareness to your senses, feeling the yarn moving in your fingers.

When you want to, change stitches. Know that this is a stitching meditation, rather than a specific project; there is no right or wrong. If you feel too aware of your thoughts, bring your awareness back to your senses, observing the colors of your yarn, your movements, the tactile sensation of the yarn in your hands.

Continue to crochet for as long as you want. When you're ready to finish, let your crochet rest in your lap as you hold it in your hands, feeling the stitches with your fingers. You can either leave your eyes open as you gaze at the stitches and yarn or close them. Then do three grounding breaths to complete your meditation.

10

CELEBRATE YOURSELF
MEDKNITATION

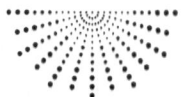

One morning, while falling down a social media rabbit hole (like we do), I saw an ad for an app that taught face Yoga. Face Yoga? As a person who has practiced Yoga for over thirty years and who wrote a book about Yoga's spiritual philosophy, and also as a person who likes to like the way she looks, this got my attention. Face Yoga! I was excited as I swiped up to learn more.

What I saw made my face fall, possibly to a level the face Yoga app creators would label a "before" photo: one of the highlights of the app's offerings was "anti-aging programs." I was amazed at how quickly this Yoga person could get supremely, very un-Yogically angry. Anti-aging? Were they kidding with this overt ageism?

Sadly, they were not. Even in these enlightened times of acceptance, ageism is a subtle tool used frequently by the makers of everything from face creams to face Yoga apps to make people feel insecure enough to buy their alleged fountain of youth. Companies and the ad agencies they employ create fear around aging, implying that youth is beauty and age is something to be avoided at all costs—at least, the cost of the product they're advertising.

I grew up with very strong female role models. My mother was a single parent who was and continues to be intelligent, talented, skillful, creative, and yes, beautiful. She had a brief career in modeling, but that's not the only thing I mean when I say she's beautiful. Her beauty radiates from her wisdom, her amazing sense of humor, her desire to help people. My mother is beautiful in all ways, inside and out.

My mother's mother, my Nana, didn't fit what are considered traditional standards of beauty, but she taught me that everyone can make the most of what they have. As a result of careful accentuation of her positive points, from her white hair to her business acumen to her conversational skills to the poetry she wrote, Nana was a stunner. People often commented on how stylish she was in both her appearance and her ability to make each individual feel like they were the most important person she had ever met. At her funeral, she needed an extra room to accommodate all the floral tributes and visitors she received.

While my mother has lived to see a wonderful, vibrant elder age, my Nana never got to be what we would consider a senior; she passed away when she was just fifty-seven. She would have been a gorgeous eighty-something because she had armloads of *joie de vivre*, either in spite of or because of the hardships she endured as a teenager supporting her entire family during the Great Depression. The joy for life is the best cosmetic you can have, along with a genuine smile.

When I saw this ad for an app with an "anti-aging" program, I was nearing my own fifty-seventh birthday. I promised myself and my Nana that if and when I got to fifty-seven, and beyond, I would honor her by living well and doing good.

Thanks to the patience that knitting and crochet have taught me, I did not take to social media hurling fireballs at this company. I considered my feelings and my thoughts on the matter. My posts on social media were a bit testy ("I find this offensive!"), but not incendiary. There would be nothing for me to apologize for or regret later. All too often, the wrath unleashed on social media leaves no room for forgiveness, or for people or companies to acknowledge mistakes and set things right. Burning somebody's virtual house down online with flaming comments only creates even more conflict, not positive change.

Apparently, I wasn't alone in my strong feelings; future ads for the face Yoga app did not mention "anti-aging." Not long after, ads for the app disappeared.

For years, I looked at photos on social media of people doing Yoga, and all I saw were young, extremely flexible people. Where were people like me, less flexible elders with silver hair? Where were the people who did Yoga in their wheelchairs? Where were people of other colors and sizes? Gradually, I began to see more diversity, though still not as many older people.

Ageism is not as bad as it used to be, but it's not as good as it could be, which would be if it were gone entirely from our culture. Chances are you may watch TV or scroll through social media and see mostly people under forty, sometimes under thirty. If you're over these ages, sometimes by decades, you can feel left out. "Where are the websites and magazines for me?" my mother asks. "Do they think I stopped caring about fashion and makeup and life at forty?"

Not everyone finds joy in getting older. I'm not exactly thrilled to feel pain in my knees, or the creaks I hear when I stretch in the morning. ("The warranty expires after fifty," my husband jokes.) But because my Nana was gone at such a relatively young age, and my beautiful friend Marnie passed away a week before her thirty-fifth birthday, I take my wrinkles and achy knees with a truckload of salt. I do celebrate getting older—not every part of it, but the fact that I'm here to make good soup and ugly sweaters and hopefully do some kindnesses. One of the things I love about the fiber arts is that I see lots of beautiful elders making things and teaching younger people about life and living well. That's something to be celebrated.

CELEBRATE YOURSELF medKNITATION

Tools: your meditative project.

Before we begin, let's remember one thing: Whatever age you are, you're beautiful!

Step 1: Follow the basic pattern for medKNITation (page 24).

Step 2: For a few moments, let your awareness rest gently on your natural breathing. Think of your breathing as being like stitches, one stitch moving into the next, one breath moving into the next. These stitches and breaths create the beautiful garment that is you.

Step 3: Bring your awareness to your stitching. Though you may have been making the motions that create stitches for so long that they're automatic, slow down a bit. Notice each motion that goes into making a stitch.

Notice the feeling of the yarn as it moves through your fingers. Notice the feelings and sensations in your fingers and hands.

Step 4: Bring to mind the project in your hands, and the projects you've created before. With each project, you have built experience and wisdom. You've learned about yourself. You are resilient. You have teachings to share, and you are teachable. There's great value in your life experience, and in you!

Our physical beings, our bodies, change over time, but physicality is not the measure of our worth. We honor our bodies and all they do for us. Each day, each moment, our bodies perform miracles, no matter what age or state they're in.

Through meditation, by observing without judgment, we view aging differently, as neither "good" nor "bad"; it just is. We celebrate our bodies. We celebrate our minds. We celebrate our spirits. We celebrate our projects and each thing we accomplish, from sharing kind words to acts on our own and others' behalf. We celebrate life.

Continue stitching for however long you like. When you're ready to finish, set your project in your lap, close your eyes, bring your awareness to your breathing, and do three grounding breaths to complete your meditation.

11

SERENITY MEDKNITATION

Forgiveness—the word, the concept, the act—is a powerful proposition. Forgiveness is high on the list of spiritual and religious achievements. "To err is human, to forgive, divine," as the saying goes. Finding the capacity within ourselves for forgiveness isn't just admirable, it's empowering. When we can do it, we've managed to rise above (hopefully not in an egotistical way) and be our best selves.

There are incredible stories of people forgiving wrongs that can't be undone; the Amish are well known for this. We admire people who can do this and are inspired by them. Yet when it comes to us, to the wrongs we've suffered, we may not be so quick to be divine. At times, I myself have opted to be decidedly un-divine about not forgiving. Even those with strong faith may find forgiveness in some situations difficult, if not impossible, but they still long for the healing that forgiveness can bring.

Why do we even need to forgive? Aren't there some wrongs in life that just can't be forgiven? That's up to the individual. For me, forgiveness hasn't been about being divine—that's too lofty a goal for me—but about being able to move on. Not forgiving people keeps me trapped in a resentment that stunts my growth. Not finding some level of forgiveness saps my serenity the way kryptonite makes Superman feel very un-super. I feel awful whenever thoughts about the hurtful situation come up again, which they will, because they're unresolved.

Some knitting problems confound us in the moment. When trying out a new pattern, something comes up that stops any further progress, other than undoing the whole thing and starting over. I've had this happen when graduating from simple knitting projects like scarves to more challenging ones like sweaters, which are full of new types of stitches, checking for fit and ease (which can induce fits and aren't easy), and sewing all the pieces together. You may have to use the complex kitchener stitch, which can make even seasoned knitters throw up their hands in frustration. Not finding a way to work with these challenges kept me at a beginner level, churning out scarf after simple rectangular scarf. Not being able to find forgiveness for people did the same thing; I felt stuck and couldn't move on.

When stumped by a challenge, sometimes the solution is setting the complicated project aside and working with something simpler. Then, during the calm of knitting, a new approach reveals itself. That can translate outside of knitting, too. If we can't forgive a harm that's been done, maybe we can consider a different approach.

The definition of forgiveness is to "stop feeling angry or resentful toward (someone) for an offense, flaw, or mistake," according to Oxford Languages. Read that again; it's not what you thought forgiveness meant, right? Forgiveness is often shown in movies and documentaries as an act of extreme kindness, the forgiver hugging the person being forgiven, even becoming a friend or mentor to them. But the definition says forgiveness means to stop feeling anger or resentment (from the old French *resentir*, meaning "to feel again"— those unresolved feelings that keep coming back). When I read this definition, I thought, *Wow, I don't have to* love *the person who did me harm.* Forgiveness could mean what the definition says, making the decision to stop being angry at them. Hugging is optional.

I've had friendships I thought would last a lifetime end abruptly, without explanation, but the resentful hurt I felt about it lasted even longer than the friendship. I thought my teachers in art school had been unjust and uncaring—and I kept feeling that way since high school, which was a *very* long time ago. That resentment kept me from drawing, something I love and that is a part of me, for decades. See what I mean about how resentment can stunt growth? I cut myself off from happiness because I had a lofty idea of forgiveness when all along it was in my power to make a decision to stop being angry and move on.

Forgiveness is up to the person doing the forgiving. Some people see it as an act of grace and a gift they bestow on the person they're forgiving. Others may feel there are harms too great to even consider forgiveness. After learning the definition of forgiveness, I took forgiving on a case-by-case basis. In some situations, I forgave the person. In others, I made a decision that the harm done to me would not hold me back in any way. Is that forgiveness? I think of it as debt cancellation. The issue gets no more of my attention. I'm busy putting my energy toward the good parts of my life. My serenity is restored.

Knitting is a space we create in which we can feel the peace of being our true selves, and in those serene moments, we can contemplate new approaches to thorny problems. The choice of a solution is up to each person, according to their comfort level. This meditation is about being in that safe and comfortable space. Maybe you'll find a solution to that challenging knitting problem that won't let you move on until you figure it out, and maybe you'll find a definition of forgiveness that works for you. Either way, remember that no one can take your serenity away from you. That's yours to keep and nurture, feeling it grow with every stitch.

SERENITY medKNITation

Tools: your meditative project.

Step 1: Follow the basic pattern for medKNITation (page 24).

Step 2: For a few moments, let your awareness rest on your natural breathing. Notice the soothing rhythm of your breathing, one breath looping into the next.

Step 3: Begin stitching and move your awareness to that. Slow down a bit. Notice each motion that goes into making a stitch, the feeling of the yarn as it moves through your fingers, the movements of your fingers and hands.

Step 4: Allow yourself to contemplate forgiveness. Now that you know there are variations on that idea, move your precious life energy away from the harm done and toward the idea of moving on from whatever has been holding you back. Think of where you want to spend your precious life energy.

Using your powers of visualization, imagine two projects in your mind. One is your serenity, a sense of peace within yourself. The other is resentment, an ugly sweater that doesn't fit, in colors you don't like. Which project would you rather spend your time and precious life energy on?

Imagine yourself folding that resentment sweater up, tucking it gently in a box, and placing that box somewhere out of the way. Now you're free to move on to working with your beautiful serenity project, which is in your favorite colors, each stitch made with love.

Continue stitching for however long feels right to you. When you're ready to finish, set your project in your lap, close your eyes if you like, and bring your awareness to your breathing. When you're ready, do three grounding breaths to complete your meditation practice.

12

"I DON'T KNOW" MEDKNITATION

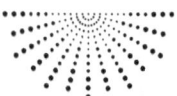

Being at ease with not knowing is crucial for answers to come to you.

— ECKHART TOLLE

When my friend Francesco had a diving accident that left him paralyzed from the shoulders down, he had more than a few visitors who said, "Everything happens for a reason." These people loved Fran, and he knew they meant well. Thinking there was some divine purpose to his accident made people more comfortable with this sudden turn of events—everyone, that is, except the person most affected by the events. The thought that there was some reason behind the accident really upset Fran.

What motivated these well-meaning folks to express this belief was the question of why bad things happen to good people. They just weren't comfortable with not knowing an answer, or the thought that there might not even be an answer as we think of it.

After one such visit, during which a very nice person assured Fran that there was a plan for him, stating confidently that this was why he'd had this accident, Fran looked at me with exasperation. "What possible reason could there be for me being in a wheelchair?" he asked.

Imagine yourself sitting in front of a twenty-three-year-old who went from being a sporty, fit runner with an easy life of doing whatever he wanted ahead of him to being in a wheelchair, unable to move anything below his shoulders. Maybe you've been in a similar situation, where some unforeseen event has happened, and everyone is struggling to make sense of it all. But this is more than a situation; it's an opportunity to try to help people deal with what's happened. That's what those well-meaning people who insisted there was a reason for Fran's accident were doing. When Francesco gave me this opportunity, I initially thought that maybe all the spirituality and philosophy I'd studied would finally come in handy in a meaningful way, and I could say something profound that would make him feel better.

If there was a divine plan at work here, the only one I could see was for me to be honest. I looked at Fran and said, "I don't know."

I told him that I didn't know if there was a reason or not for the accident to have happened. The only thing I did know is that people seem to feel more comfortable thinking there are reasons for everything, because they're not comfortable not knowing.

We don't have to be faced with devastating events to become uncomfortable with not knowing why something happened or didn't happen. We've all seen our carefully made plans come undone, like dropping a stitch and watching it unravel all the way down that meticulously knitted sweater. In the moment, it's hard to look at the possible bright side of not marrying the person you thought you were in love with, or of losing a job, or not getting the "perfect house." If someone even hints that things might work out better than our plans that fell through, we're pretty certain they won't—which is another attempt at knowing. Even deciding something is bad seems safer than saying, "I don't know."

Not everything works out in our favor, or the favor of someone we love. Bad things happen to good people all the time. We wonder why, and we rarely get clear answers; we have to come to our own. Those answers can include not knowing and accepting that.

The Buddha, before enlightenment, had been a prince living an enviable, comfort-filled life free from unpleasantness; his parents saw to that. One day, the young prince sneaked out of the palace and saw

SUZAN COLÓN

all the things he'd been shielded from—loss, illness, struggle, death. Most of all, he saw suffering, and he began a spiritual quest to find solutions for suffering.

While the Buddha never offered answers about why bad things happen to good people, he began a philosophy that has endured for thousands of years by coming to a simple conclusion: pain in life is inevitable, but suffering over that pain is optional.

Maybe what causes some of our suffering is our need to know, to become attached to our plans and ideas. Making plans is necessary in many parts of life. Within these plans, it's also a good idea to have some flexibility if those plans change. When I look back on some of the things I thought I wanted, I'm grateful for unanswered prayers. Many of the plans that didn't go the way I wanted them to at the time led to much, much better situations. If I'd known everything, or stuck rigidly to my plans, these better outcomes, like being married to the love of my life, might not have happened. When I look back on these times of change in my carefully knitted plans, I see how I had to occupy a space, comfortable or not, with not knowing why the change happened, or what might happen from there. Once I accepted that, I could go through the pain, but I wasn't suffering.

As for Francesco, he didn't waste much time or his precious life energy on suffering. He felt his feelings so he could get used to this big change in his life. Then he started a skincare company, Clark's Botanicals, became a spokesperson for the Christopher and Dana Reeve Foundation, and got married and had two children—all while in his wheelchair. He may wonder from time to time if there's some reason for his accident, but he's okay with not knowing. He's too busy, and happy, making new plans.

"I Don't Know" medKNITation

Tools: your meditative project.

Step 1: Follow the basic pattern for medKNITation (page 24).
Step 2: For a few moments, let your awareness rest on your

breathing. Observe your inhalations and exhalations as they happen. You may notice that your breathing is even, almost predictable, for a while. Then your body may decide it wants a deeper breath. Breathing is both automatic, happening on its own while we sleep and do other things, and we can also change it by choosing to take a deep breath. Take a deep breath consciously here. Let it out slowly.

Step 3: Bring your awareness to your stitching, slowing your movements slightly. If you've been knitting for a while, you're aware of the soothing repetition of movements. Enjoy them.

Notice the feeling of the yarn as it moves through your fingers. Notice the sensations in your fingers and hands. Follow the yarn as it loops through previous loops.

As a knitter, you know that no matter how long you've been knitting, you may drop a stitch, lose count of stitches or rows, or something else unforeseen may occur in your project. These things have happened, you've fixed what you could, and you kept knitting, looking forward to each new project.

Step 4: Contemplate not knowing why your plans changed, and not knowing what's going to happen. We've all had experience with that. When we look back on these experiences, we're looking back from having gotten through that. Maybe not knowing was uncomfortable. Maybe you practiced acceptance.

However you got through it, you have experience to draw on for the next time it happens. Contemplate the idea that there will be changes in life, and that some of them will be painful, but that suffering is optional.

Continue stitching for however long you want. When you're ready to finish this meditation, set your project in your lap. Close your eyes and bring your awareness to your breathing. Do three grounding breaths to complete your meditation practice.

13

INTENTION MEDKNITATION

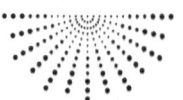

Sometimes knitters will find a pattern, go to the yarn shop, get the materials necessary for the project, and begin happily stitching away. Other times, we go to the yarn shop, fall in love with some spectacular yarn we've never seen before, and buy some on the spot. We get it home, we smoosh it and sigh over the color and texture, and then we wonder what we're going to do with it. Without an intention, that new yarn we were so excited about can sit in our stash for years. (Note to knitters with sizable stashes: I'm not implying that there's a problem with that.)

So much in life is goal-oriented. Children learn at school that the goal is to get good grades, and only recently are adults learning that testing methods for children are not one-size-fits-all; a child could be brilliant and simply not test well, or learn better through visual, rather than written, methods. Our jobs are focused on goals; the point is to make profit, or carry out the company's mission. In our personal lives, we start thinking about more goals around December in the form of New Year's Resolutions. Recently, I've heard people saying they don't bother making those anymore, since they usually fail by February. This is why I started leaning toward the idea of setting intentions.

I became aware of intentions in Yoga classes, when teachers would say, during the quiet, calm beginning, that we could set an intention for our practice. They said that if someone in our lives needed some extra love or support, our intention could be to send it to them, or to offer our practice in honor of them. Intentions sounded like a gentle meeting of prayer and a goal. I would be able to take some action while remembering that life unfolds as it does, requiring flexibility with expectations and desires.

Goals and resolutions came with a hard line of success or failure that was discouraging. With intentions, that line was softer and less clearly defined. Setting an intention was like aiming an arrow in a general direction; the point was not that it land precisely, but to let it fly.

The broad approach of intentions felt like doing something and watching it unfold, rather than getting something done in the fastest, most efficient way possible, which sometimes didn't work out well. As a knitter, this was something I could relate to. We usually want to power through a project when it's a gift meant for a specific date, like a birthday. We'd like to get the baby blanket done before the kid goes off to college! Otherwise, knitting is like setting an intention. We set out to make a sweater, work toward that, and see what happens.

I went to a new yarn shop one day, a tiny one that specialized in small batches of hand-spun, hand-dyed yarn by independent yarn makers. This stuff wasn't going to be available online or at the chain craft store. Even though I had plenty of yarn and projects in process at home, I bought two skeins of a cheery, bright yellow yarn speckled with pink and blue flecks. Later, I found a pattern for a short-sleeved sweater, the kind you can wear for about three days in spring before it gets too hot and three days in fall before it gets too cold. (Of course, I bought the pattern immediately.) My intention was to make this sweater from that yarn.

That was about three years ago. The work was slow but enjoyable, the colors becoming more vivid as the garment grew, and somewhere along the yoke I began to wonder whether I even looked good in yellow. Carefully, after running a lifeline of scrap yarn through the many stitches, I took what I had off the needles and tried it on. Not only were this color and I not a match made in yarn heaven, but I'd misread the instructions somewhere and now had not a sweater yoke but the beginnings of a knitted canoe.

Was this a failure? Maybe, but I didn't feel discouraged. As I unraveled the project, watching it become smaller, the initial intention grew: I hadn't just set out to make a sweater, I'd explored a new yarn shop, tried out a new type of yarn, worked with a new pattern. I'd set out to knit, and I looked back on many happy hours of stitching away. My intention shifted to giving the yarn to a friend who does look good in yellow, and who, from knitting and living, has learned that trees flexible enough to bend in the changing wind have a better time of it than rigid ones.

Making resolutions and setting goals have their place, and another option is to try setting intentions that give your ideas and plans room to grow from cocoon to butterfly, enjoying the changes along the way.

INTENTION medKNITATION

Tools: your meditative project, and your journal and a pen.

Step 1: Follow the basic pattern for medKNITation (page 24).

Step 2: Let your awareness rest gently on your breathing, just noticing. Allow your focus on your inhalations and exhalations take you inward for a few minutes.

Step 3: Bring your awareness to your stitching. Though you may have been making the motions that create stitches for so long that they're automatic, slow down. Notice each motion that goes into making a stitch, the feeling of the yarn as it moves through your fingers.

Step 4: You may have come into this meditation with an intention already in mind. If so, now that you're in a relaxed state of open-mindedness, see how that intention fits for you. Ask yourself if you'd like to modify it in any way.

If you came to this meditation with a desire to achieve something, but not a specific intention, see if one comes to you now. What would make this plan feel right, and doable, for you? Think of the flexibility of yarn. We can be flexible in our plans for ourselves, too.

Hold your intention in your mind for a few moments, enjoying the possibilities and potential of the intention. Understand that this may come to pass in different ways than you envision or plan; just as with a knitting project, we can adjust as we go along.

When the feeling of the intention is right for you, state your intention aloud.

Continue stitching for however long is comfortable for you. When you're ready to finish this session, set your project in your lap. Close your eyes and bring your awareness to your breathing. Do three grounding breaths to complete your meditation.

14

"LET IT BE" MEDKNITATION

The advice we get from people, pop culture, self-help gurus, songs, the media, and seemingly everyone about unresolved matters that stay in our hearts and minds like knots that can't be undone is to "Let it go." These problems—events that didn't go the way we'd hoped, arguments, resentments, regrets—take up energy and our most precious resources, our time and attention. "Just let it go," we hear again and again, and yet there are no instructions as to *how* to untie those knots that keep us bound in the event, no matter how long ago it may have happened.

When we're knitting, we like a pattern of instructions. I wanted some instructions on how to let things go. I found someone who made a small tweak to the idea that changed everything, like learning there's a misprint in the pattern and correcting it.

Nick Hobson, Chief Behavioral Scientist at Apex Scoring Solutions, conducted a study in which five hundred participants were asked to recall a difficult time within the past two years when they were very stressed, and to focus on how they felt for three minutes. One part of the group was given no instruction other than to observe their feelings. Another part was instructed to repeat the mantra "Let it go" during the three minutes. The last group was told to repeat the mantra "Let it be."

The people in the first group had to bear their feelings. The "Let it go" group said they felt a fairly significant decrease in bad feelings. Yet the group focusing on "Let it be" felt much better, with a forty-five percent decrease in anxiety. The reason? Hobson's theory is that letting something *be* requires far less effort than trying to let something go. The situation is there, but it's reduced to a fact, rather than you trying to summon the effort to pretend it didn't hurt.

This is similar to practicing acceptance, but a little more pro-active. While it's true that accepting situations and our feelings about them is practical, it's sometimes not as helpful as it could be because it lacks an action we can take. The idea of using the mantra "Let it be" is empowering. We can make the choice to not become entangled in the situation and the emotions that come with it. By choosing to let something be, we're saying, "Yes, that happened, but I don't need to go there again." We don't have to pretend we didn't feel the way we felt, but we don't have to feel the emotions all over again. We can, as Hobson suggested, let it be. Three simple words that truly are, as Paul McCartney wrote, words of wisdom.

As with knitting's more complex stitches, or any other new learning experience, this exercise takes practice. With time, patience, and compassion, by letting the issues residing in our minds and hearts to just be, the knots of emotions can ease themselves open, and we may find our relationship with them transformed—and ourselves along with them.

"LET IT BE" medKNITation

Tools: Your meditative project.

You may already have some unresolved issue, such as an argument with a friend or family member, problem at work, or some other stressful situation that keeps coming up in your mind to use during this medKNITation. My suggestion would be to choose a small matter, not your most stressful situation, to practice with; this will be more manageable. If you don't have anything bothering you right now—lucky you!—skip this meditation until you need it.

Step 1: Follow the basic pattern for medKNITation (page 24).

Step 2: For a few moments, let your awareness rest gently on your natural breathing. Think of each breath as a new beginning.

Step 3: The issue you've had on your mind will probably come up without much effort. Allow it to do so, but without investing too much mental energy on it; this is not a debate about your right to feel the way you have felt, nor an excuse to rehash the details. This is a meditation practice. Framing it that way can give you some distance from it.

Bring your awareness to your stitching. Though you may have been making the motions that create stitches for so long that they are automatic, slow down a bit. Notice each motion that goes into making a stitch. Notice the feeling of the yarn as it moves through your fingers. Notice the sensations in your fingers and hands.

Follow the yarn as it loops through previous loops, a single strand creating woven mesh.

Step 4: As you find your rhythm with the stitches, silently repeat this mantra: *Let it be.*

Continue stitching for however long you want. When you're ready to finish, set your project in your lap. Close your eyes and bring your awareness to your breathing. Do three grounding breaths to complete your meditation.

Notice how you feel about the situation you brought to mind now, as opposed to the way you've felt in the past. Write about your experiences in your medKNITation journal.

15

MASSAGE MEDKNITATION

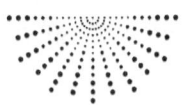

Every now and then, usually while I'm admiring a significant number of rows I've knitted, happy to see such a wide swath of fabric I've woven with my own hands, I notice my posture. Or, rather, some pain in my body reminds me to notice my posture. I've slumped down in our soft couch. My head is forward, my arms at an odd angle. My body may be twisting or bending to accommodate a cat napping in my lap. I probably look like a hunched-over shrimp.

At times like these, I wonder why I don't take my own good suggestions to get up every few rows, walk around, do a gentle hula to unkink my hips, and massage my face, which has been set in concentration for over an hour, and my hands and wrists, which have been repeating the same motions for at least two shows, or one full movie.

Knitters, artists, gamers, people who work at computers all day— we know that sitting in one place for a long time is not good for our bodies. Knitting is so relaxing and meditative that it's hard to remember to get up and move around. Next thing we know, *ouch*. In the saddest-case scenario, an injury prevents us from being able to do what we love to do. "I couldn't knit for a year because of carpal tunnel syndrome," a friend told me. "I thought I'd lose my mind."

That doesn't have to happen. Set an intention to get up and move around every few rows or every twenty minutes, whichever comes first. If setting an intention isn't enough, set an alarm on your phone to remind you. Walk around. Walk to the bathroom, to the kitchen to get more water, walk in a few circles. Stretch and move in whatever way feels good to you. (You'll also find a series of gentle movements in Section III.)

To make moving around something you'll look forward to, try this massage meditation as a reward when you sit back down again.

Massage medKNITation

Tools: those amazing digital instruments, your own hands.

Though I just gave you a big speech about getting up after sitting for a long period of time, this meditation is best done while sitting because it's so relaxing, you may want to close your eyes. Start out with the gentlest touch possible so you can explore which of the exercises feels best to you. If something doesn't feel good, don't do it. Experiment with levels of pressure and motions. Never press hard, especially on your temples.

While people usually think of meditation as sitting still, activities such as walking and knitting can be meditative. Doing these massage exercises can be the same.

Step 1: Sit up tall, with both feet on the floor. Do the three grounding breaths.

Step 2: Bring your fingertips to your head and give yourself a scalp massage. Start out with light pressure, relieving any tension that may have gathered.

Using your thumbs, locate the area at the base of your skull between your ears and your neck and massage there. Again, not too much pressure; this should feel good.

Bring your fingertips to the hinge of your jaw, in front of your ears, and massage there.

Using only your ring (fourth) fingers, which have the lightest touch of all the fingers, make slow, smoothing motions at the tops of your cheekbones.

Step 3: Now it's time to massage your hands. Use your thumb and fingers to gently massage each hand in any way that feels good to you.

Gently massage your wrists, your forearms, and your shoulders.

Bring your fingertips to your neck and upper shoulder muscles and massage them.

Step 4: To exercise the facial muscles, do the following: gently scrunch your face, imagining all your muscles moving toward the tip of your nose. Hold for one second, then release.

Open your eyes wide, open your mouth, and stretch your facial muscles. Hold for one second, and release.

Smile wide, as though you've just won a year's supply of yarn! Give a big grin, hold for one second, and release.

When you're finished with the massages and exercises, do three grounding breaths to complete the meditation. Happy knitting!

Be Happy and Smile, or Smile and Be Happy?

Both can be true. While we usually think we smile when we're happy, researchers studying facial expressions discovered that making the facial expressions associated with an emotion such as anger, happiness, or sadness could bring on the emotion, even if the subject hadn't been feeling that way before. The next time you're feeling blue, try smiling; your brain will receive a little lift, and your mood may improve.

16

PERSONAL SPACE MEDKNITATION

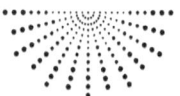

Manhattan, the heart of New York City, is actually not a very big place. It's a little over thirteen miles long and a tad over two miles at its widest point. It's also the most densely populated of the five boroughs that make up New York City; as of 2024, over 1.6 million people live on this island. On an average day, they're joined by people commuting in from surrounding areas to go to work and tourists from all over the world catching a play on Broadway or going to the many museums we have here. You might say it's a little crowded.

Growing up in New York City, as I did, you develop a certain approach to personal space: We don't expect to get much of it, so we guard what little we have. In places you know will be crowded, like the subway at rush hour, you accept the fact that you won't have much space for yourself. You put in your headphones or get out your book and pretend you're not packed like a sardine in a tin can. Sometimes, on longer train rides going out of the city, there's more space, especially in non-rush hour times. You can even get two seats to yourself so you can spread out. (This is the kind of thing New Yorkers dream about.)

Even for people who live in larger, less populated areas, the idea of personal space can be challenged in, say, a hospital waiting room, or some place or situation where you wish you had a little bubble of protection around you. This is yet another way knitting and stitching can go above and beyond the idea of a happy little pastime.

One Saturday afternoon, I set out on an hour-long train ride to visit my family. I had a snack, a book, and my project bag, and as we left Penn Station, I was all set for a peaceful trip. When we started making stops outside Manhattan, I noticed a lot of people getting on the train. A lot of young people...dressed in green. Slowly, it dawned on me: I'd forgotten this was St. Patrick's Day. In a few more stops, the train was suddenly packed. The smell of beer was everywhere, there was much hooting and hollering, and although this was a festive bunch, there's a fine line between celebrating and fighting when alcohol is involved. Being part Irish, I love St. Patrick's Day, but not all the drinking that tends to go with it. For those of us on the train who weren't drunk, the atmosphere was slightly intimidating.

I tried to keep reading, but when things started getting rowdy around me and I couldn't focus on my book, I took out the knitting I'd brought with me. Within just a few rows, a wonderful inward experience began. I was aware of the commotion around me, but it felt further away. (Nothing to be done about the smell of beer, but I noticed it less.) In moments, I felt as though a bubble was around me, creating a nice bit of distance between me and the partiers on the train. The rest of the trip was a variation on the peaceful time I'd been looking forward to.

Since then, I've had similar experiences in crowded subways, waiting rooms, and any other places where I need a little space. Knitting holds our focus, giving us a way inward that helps us create space around ourselves. The next time you feel the need to create a little personal space, take out your knitting and try this medKNITation. When I do this, I sometimes like to imagine the entire island of Manhattan knitting away peacefully.

PERSONAL SPACE medKNITATION

Tools: Any project you have on hand.

Most of the meditations in this book begin with the same basic steps. This one may seem to be out of order, but that will help you be drawn into the meditation more easily.

Step 1: With your project in hand, begin stitching.

Step 2: Engage your senses by directing your awareness to your stitching. Notice each motion of your fingers and hands that goes into making a stitch.

Notice the feeling of the yarn as it moves through your fingers. Notice the sensations in your fingers and hands.

As you work with the yarn, notice the colors, the fibers, the way the light makes a single color change hues.

Follow the yarn as it loops through previous loops, a single strand creating woven mesh. Notice the spaces between the yarn. Think of them as breathing spaces.

Step 3: When we're free from distraction, being drawn into our knitting happens effortlessly. In situations where there are distractions, you can help this focus along by directing your awareness through your senses. Use the physical sensations, the movements, the colors and feel of the yarn as anchors for your awareness, gently steering you back to what you have in your hands.

Step 4: Imagine that you're weaving a beautiful bubble of energy around yourself. You can imagine that this bubble is made of the finest, yet strongest fiber in your favorite color. This bubble is your space. Within it, you reclaim your natural sense of peace.

Continue stitching for however long you want. When you're ready to finish, set your project in your lap, close your eyes, and bring your awareness to your breathing. Do three grounding breaths to complete your meditation.

17

BLANKET OF PEACE
MEDKNITATION

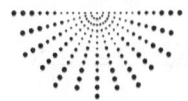

When Vogue Knitting Live went online and began doing regular virtual gatherings, I was given the gift of leading morning meditations. I loved these sessions, where people would come to our virtual space and we'd all meditate together for a while, first with our breathing, then with knitting. These were relaxed and happy times, and I always looked forward to them.

One day in February 2022, before I was scheduled to lead a morning meditation, Russia launched their unprovoked attack on Ukraine. People were shaken. How could this happen? Yet it was happening, and it was on everyone's minds. I wondered whether or not to mention this event. I thought I should acknowledge what was happening, but would it upset the meditation attendees if I did?

At times like these, I rely on the tools my wise teachers gave me. One of them was to remember to stabilize my own energy. As the person leading the meditation, people would look to me for cues, and they would be affected by my energy. I made sure to sit and do some calm breathing exercises before I logged in to the room. During that time, I recalled a meditation by beloved instructor Sharon Salzberg. In that meditation, Sharon led us in sending loving kindness to people we love, then extending it to people we liked, then to people we felt neutral about, and then even to people we disliked. Challenging! It's a wonderful exercise in seeing connection, cultivating empathy, and suspending judgment.

I love to adapt the meditations I do for the stitching community, and that morning, when people arrived in the virtual space with troubled expressions and worried minds, this meditation flowed on the spot. Whenever conflict arises, whether somewhere in the world or in my own little part of the world, I practice this meditation.

BLANKET OF PEACE medKNITATION

Tools: your meditative project. If you're working on a blanket, use that.

Remember the movie *Like Water for Chocolate*? (If you haven't seen it yet, it's well worth renting!) In that movie, there's a scene where the heroine, Tita, begins making a blanket that then grows to amazing proportions. That's what I envision when I do this meditation.

Step 1: Follow the basic pattern for medKNITation (page 24).

Step 2: Engage your senses by directing your awareness to your stitching. Notice each motion of your fingers and hands that goes into making a stitch.

Notice the feeling of the yarn as it moves through your fingers. Notice the sensations in your fingers and hands.

Step 3: Imagine you're making a blanket that has the power to create a feeling of peace. It's soft, made of very strong, resilient yarn in soothing colors. Imagine being surrounded by that blanket.

As you stitch, visualize the blanket growing, becoming big enough to wrap around the people and animals you love most.

Now imagine the blanket of peace extending to wrap around more people—your friends, family, neighborhood. This magical blanket grows large enough to encircle your town, your city, even your state.

As you stitch, imagine your blanket growing to extend further, beyond the horizon, much farther than you can see, bringing that wonderful sense of peace to all who need it.

Continue stitching for as long as you'd like. When you're ready to finish, set your project in your lap, close your eyes, and bring your awareness to your breathing. Remember your breathing meditation: breathe in peace, and breathe out peace.

Do three grounding breaths to complete your meditation, knowing that the peace you sent out into the world endures.

18

COMPLETED PROJECT
MEDKNITATION

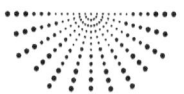

Ah, the allure of the crocheted granny square. The series of organized loops looked intimidating at first, but when I finally tried to make one with some thick, forgiving yarn, I was a convert. I wanted to make granny squares for an entire summer, and that's about what it takes to make a decent-sized granny square throw. Once I had enough of them, I began seaming them together.

Even though each square looked the same, I could tell when I'd made them from the tension in the stitches. Some had an even feel to them, and I knew these calm squares had been made as meditation, or while watching movies with my husband. Other squares had tight or uneven stitches, and I knew those had been made while traveling to my biological father's house after his diagnosis of colon cancer. Those squares gave me a great deal of relief; just having something to do with my hands, and doing the same thing over and over, had been soothing and stabilizing.

There were a lot of emotions in these squares, I thought as I stitched them together. A lot of life.

The following summer, I made my father a chemo hat. The idea of doing this constructive, useful project only occurred to me the day I was set to go visit for his birthday. I stitched madly on the train, using a pattern I knew would knit up quickly, and I stitched during the afternoon with my father, stepmother, and sisters, even while singing "Happy Birthday." Toward the end, when I was decreasing stitches at the crown and getting more and more anxious about the time, and the reason for the hat, I actually broke one of my bamboo circular needles.

Today, I have that hat. I think about that day whenever I wear it, and about why I have it back. I completed the project in time for my father to use it, and, the following summer, he no longer needed it. His project, his life, was completed.

There are many who believe that our emotions have powerful vibrations that can be imbued into the projects we make. This is the intention in Prayer Shawls, which are created while the maker focuses on prayers that will help the recipient of the shawl.

You may have a project you've been making for someone else, or one you've been making for yourself, maybe to prove to yourself that you could make something that tested your knitting skills, or to help you through a difficult time. Even though you're done with the project, you may not be done with the emotions that were woven into it. With this meditation, you can truly complete it and honor its purpose.

MED**KNIT**ATION FOR A COMPLETED PROJECT

Tools: a finished project that's for you, or for someone else.

Step 1: Find a comfortable seat, preferably in a quiet place. Ground and center yourself.

Step 2: For a few moments, let your awareness rest on your natural breathing pattern.

Step 3: Gently open your eyes and look at your project. Imagine your emotions flowing from your hands into the project.

If you were feeling happiness as you made this, your happiness goes into it.

If you made this to relieve anxiety, your feelings of calm and stability go into this project.

If you were feeling pain or sorrow, know that the act of creating transforms your sorrow and pain into strength. Your strength goes into this project.

If you were making this project to learn something new, your willingness to grow and your playful curiosity go into this project.

Step 4: Bring the project to your chest and hold it there. You may be able to feel your heart beating into your project.

Now bring to your mind and heart whatever you want to put into this project. Love. Good health. Joy. Happiness. Peace. Serenity. Open-mindedness. Willingness. Compassion. Strength. Add anything specific you want the person or being, if it's for a pet, to receive with this gift. If the project is for yourself, pour the love you would wish for yourself into this project.

Feel the wonderful emotions you want to put into the project, then inhale and exhale, breathing your inspiration into it.

When you're ready to finish your meditation, let the project rest in your lap. Bring your awareness back to your breath, observing the pattern of inhalation into exhalation into inhalation, and so on. Close the meditation with three grounding breaths.

19

"LET ME KNIT ON THAT" MEDKNITATION

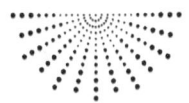

In the early days of in-person medKNITation sessions at Knitty City, I was learning as much as much as I was teaching. After leading the meditations, I would ask people about their experiences. Sometimes they were quiet, still in that calm place that knitting in silence can create. Others would share how this was something they wanted to make a regular practice.

On one of these evenings, a knitter I hadn't met before had a different kind of smile on her face after the meditation. When I asked about her experience, she said that this was familiar to her, and it had a purpose beyond relaxation. "My daughter will come to me with a problem," the woman said, "and she'll ask, 'Mom, what do you think I should do?' And I tell her, 'Well, let me knit on that for a while.'" She concluded by saying that usually, a solution to the problem would surface while she sat and knitted quietly. The rest of us were wide-eyed: here was something we might have experienced before, but maybe by accident. Now it was a tool we could use intentionally.

In recent years, we've been hearing about the many benefits of knitting. Blood pressure lowers, relaxation increases, and knitters experience a feeling similar to Yoga's deep relaxation. Included among the benefits was an improvement in creative thinking. An expert questioned that benefit, saying this was hard to measure; one would have to prove that a person was not a very creative thinker before knitting, and then find a scientifically measurable way to show that they'd suddenly become a veritable problem-solving whiz after a few rows of stockinette. The evidence on the improved creative thinking benefit remained anecdotal.

This doesn't mean it isn't true. As the person who said "Let me knit on that" pointed out, this worked for her, and probably does for many people—maybe you, too. It's possible that, without intending to solve a problem, you sat down to knit for a while to de-stress from a problem, and while working on that gloriously stripey sock, a solution popped into your mind. Even though a team of researchers wasn't there to apply electrodes to your head and watch your brainwaves shimmy, that doesn't mean it didn't work; it means science hasn't gotten around to measuring it yet. Who knows, there may be some team of yarn-obsessed scientists somewhere saying, "There's really something to this knitting-creative thinking theory!"

Until that wonderful team gets to work, I have no problem with doing my own experiments on this, and I invite you to join the very unofficial research group and try it yourself.

"LET ME KNIT ON THAT" medKNITation

Tools: your meditative project.

Unlike other meditations, where you leave a problem, question, or other thoughts outside of the meditation session, now you're bringing that question into the meditation with you. Rather than focusing on specifics, just have the question or situation in mind. Think of it as waiting patiently for solution options to present themselves.

Step 1: Follow the basic pattern for medKNITation (page 24).
Step 2: For a few moments, let your awareness rest gently on your

natural breathing. You don't have to alter your breath in any way. Simply observe your breathing.

Step 3: Begin stitching, more slowly than you usually do. Notice each motion that goes into making a stitch and the feeling of the yarn as it moves through your fingers.

Notice, without too much effort, the pattern of loop into loop, one following the next in a soothing order.

Step 4: Continue knitting. At some point you may be aware that your mind, now calmer, is considering the question or problem. You may be exploring options that were not immediately apparent. You don't need to try to stop thinking; this is meditative, creative, solution-oriented thinking. The idea is to knit while contemplating the situation. Let your mind wander.

If nothing is coming to you, rest your awareness on your breathing for a few moments, and then on your knitting. There's no need to force anything. Breathe. Knit. Relax. Repeat. Maybe this is the solution, and all that needs to be done for now.

Continue stitching for however long you want. When you're ready to stop, set your project in your lap, close your eyes, and bring your awareness back to your breathing. Do three grounding breaths to complete your meditation.

A problem, and a creative idea: #TenForTarot

One of my examples of "Let me knit on that" came in 2019, when our local foodbank was sending out an SOS for extra donations. My husband and I make regular donations, so we upped the amount, but our area wasn't alone. People all over the country were experiencing food insecurity (defined as not knowing where your next meal will come from) in record numbers. How could I help more? I used the "Let me knit on this" meditation, and what came to me was a fun way to fundraise: #TenForTarot.

I've been reading Tarot cards for years. My readings were mostly for myself, but during this meditation, I saw that readings could be turned into feedings! The idea that revealed itself during the meditation was simple: I offered a three-card Tarot reading in exchange for a ten-dollar donation to Feeding America, which sends funds to the neediest food banks in the nation. The donor could also send their ten Tarot bucks (or more, if they wanted) to their local food bank or animal shelter. People sent the money directly to the charity of their choice, showed me a screenshot of their donation receipt (with their financial info blanked out), and I pulled three cards for them. Given the financial crisis that came with the pandemic, I ended up doing #TenForTarot four years in a row. Thankfully, I was joined by other Tarot readers, so I wasn't overwhelmed by requests! Together, the wonderful donors we read for raised enough money for thousands of meals and other supplies to help people and animals in need.

This was further proof of that creative thinking benefit, as well as showing that the "Let me knit on this" meditation really works. Try it and see!

2 0

POSITIVE ENERGY
MEDKNITATION

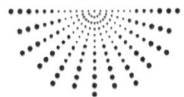

Whatever you're looking for, you can find it on social media. If you want inspiration for projects, creative knitting tricks, or fun pet videos, social media will show it to you. Unfortunately, there's also no shortage of negative opinions, bad news, and conflict. Even worse, if someone reads a negative story or comments on it, their social media feed becomes filled with similarly terrible news. Not everyone realizes that social media algorithms are designed to measure interest, not what's nice and what's upsetting. Click "like" on anything, or even just pause to read a post, and the algorithm takes note and gives you more of the same. (Sadly, social media analysis shows that more people engage with posts that make them angry than they do with posts about things they like.)

The opposite is also true. Click or read good news, and you'll find more of it. Stories of people coming up with ingenious ideas to help others, posts about kindness and optimism—those are out there too. All we have to do is seek them, and they'll find us.

Whenever friends and family tell me about something awful they saw on social media and that the world is becoming a terrible place, I remind them that their algorithm has become poisoned, and then I tell them the story of my friend Stacy Wiener.

Back when Stacy was a new volunteer at her local food bank, she asked her supervisor why there were so many requests from the food bank's clients for soap and other toiletries. "People can't use their food stamps to get soap, toothpaste, deodorant, or any other toiletries," the supervisor explained. While the food bank was able to give out things to eat, they didn't have soap—one of the most basic of daily needs—and the clients were unable to obtain any with their food stamps.

There were a few ways Stacy could have dealt with this information. One was to feel sorry for the clients and ruminate about how life is unfair and the system is flawed. Another was to buy a lot of soap and hand it out to the clients at her food bank—but what about other people at food banks all over the nation?

Then Stacy found another option. A knitter and crocheter, Stacy made a pattern for a small pouch with a loop. A bar of soap could be put into the pouch, and the pouch itself, being made of cotton yarn, would double as a washcloth. She began making these sacks—or S.A.C.K.s, short for Supporting A Community with Kindness—and enlisting friends to make them too. Then, strangers. Then, anyone and everyone who could make a sack, or a few, or a hundred.

As news of Soap S.A.C.K.s spread, Stacy encouraged makers to donate them to their own local food banks, as well as to shelters for people without homes and people fleeing domestic violence, veterans' homes, LGBTQ+ organizations, sites of disasters—anywhere someone might need to engage in the simple act of maintaining dignity and a sense of normalcy with a good scrub.

The ingenious idea, and the wonderful feeling of being able to help others, spread to every state in America, and then to other continents. Stacy got major corporations to donate soap and yarn for the project. And Soap S.A.C.K.s don't just help the recipients. Stacy told me the story of a person who had been bedridden with depression; they found out about Soap S.A.C.K.s, started making them, and told Stacy that making the sacks had given them a feeling of purpose—and told her in person, at a donation drop-off site. Over 700,000 sacks filled with soap and other basic toiletries have been given out globally. Each one is made with care and kindness.

There may be a lot of division in this country and in the world, but there's also a lot of kindness and hope. There are solid reasons to be optimistic, and when we to do our part to help others, we become that optimism that inspires others to do good, too. Be the human version of a social media algorithm—give more of the good you're looking for in the world.

POSITIVE ENERGY medKNITation

Tools: a meditative project (such as a Soap S.A.C.K.! For free Soap S.A.C.K.s patterns, and information on how to make sacks for your own community, visit www.soapsacks.com).

We have the ability to shift our energy from focusing on the negative to the good we can do. Even the smallest action, such as a smile and a few kind words, can be more meaningful than we know. This medKNITation can help you shift your perspective to the positive—and who knows what good can come from that?

Read through the meditation first. Then, begin your medKNITation, stitching as you allow the message to flow through your consciousness. You don't have to remember the exact wording; the general sentiment will do just fine.

Step 1: Follow the basic pattern for medKNITation (page 24).

Step 2: For a few moments, let your awareness rest gently on your breathing, noticing each inhalation flowing into each exhalation.

Step 3: Bring your awareness to your stitching, going slowly, enjoying the movements of your hands and fingers, the feeling of the yarn between your fingers.

Step 4: Say the following to yourself, silently or aloud:

My energy is bright and beautiful.
My energy is strong and light.
My energy is precious, and I spend it wisely.

My energy is useful.
My energy is kind.
My energy is meaningful and helpful.

My energy does so much good.
My energy is beautiful and bright, strong and light.
My energy brings good to the world.

Repeat as much as you want. Feel free to release the wording, while continuing to hold the feeling, for as long as you like. Then, set your project in your lap. Close your eyes and bring your awareness to your breathing. When you're ready, do three grounding breaths to complete your meditation practice.

2 1

RESTART YOUR DAY
MEDKNITATION

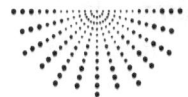

This day was not going the way I'd planned.

When I woke up, I was looking forward to a full day of writing this book, doing an Instagram Live with a friend, and checking off a bunch of boxes on my to-do list. As I made my oat milk matcha, though, I started reflecting on the previous evening. Something I'd said to a friend seemed to have landed the wrong way. I had no proof of that, but the possibility was like a dripping faucet, something I couldn't ignore. Then there was a post on social media that bothered me. My mood turned quickly, and from then on, nothing seemed to go right.

Only a few degrees of change are necessary for a cruise ship to make a big, wide turn, and that turn can be continuing on course or heading blindly out to sea. It's the same with mood. First thing in the morning, I was fine. An hour later, I was wildly off course.

Years ago, I heard about a wonderful concept: you can restart your day. During a day that isn't going well, you can decide to start over, any time until 11:59 pm (when you automatically get a new day). Wow! If the day wasn't going well, I didn't have to sit in the bad feeling and know that everything I did would be clouded with that funk. I could just press the reset button and restart the day!

Working with yarn taught me the same thing. The night before this not-great day, I'd started to crochet a new cat bed. This soft little mat of woven yarn was meant to fit a specific box, but it took me several tries to get the size right. Each time, I'd made it too big, or too small, or the stitch was too airy and loose; something had gone wrong. And I'd unravel the work and restart. I didn't dwell on the mistakes. The act of beginning again was like an eraser wiping a scribbled-on chalkboard clean (or, for a modern version, pressing the "delete" button).

I've had to restart my day many times, sometimes well into the evening. Each time, I feel gratitude that the rest of the day, even if there's only one minute left to it, can be better.

RESTART YOUR DAY medKNITation

Tools: your meditative project.

Step 1: Follow the basic pattern for medKNITation (page 24).

Step 2: For a few moments, let your awareness rest gently on your breathing. Think of each breath as a new beginning, a fresh start.

Step 3: Bring your awareness to your stitching, going a bit more slowly than you usually do. Notice the motions that go into making each stitch, the yarn moving through your fingers, the needles or hook in your hands.

Step 4: Pause, close your eyes for a moment, and imagine you're feeling the warmth of the morning sun on your face, enjoying the start of a fresh, new day.

Take three cleansing breaths, releasing whatever came before this moment.

Bring your awareness back to your stitching. Notice each new stitch, each fresh beginning of a row. Let your stitching ease you into your new day.

Continue stitching for however long feels right to you. When you're ready to finish, set your project in your lap, close your eyes, and bring your awareness to your breathing. Do three grounding breaths to complete your meditation practice.

2 2

AFFIRMATION MEDKNITATION

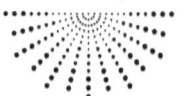

One morning, I was having trouble getting out of bed. I don't mean there was anything physically wrong with me; I could've complained of minor aches and creakiness, but that would've been stretching the truth in search of an explanation. The problem was not in my body, but in my mind. The closest I could come to finding a reason for my inability to get out of bed was that I'd developed a case of the blahs.

I've been through times like this before. Generally, whenever I have something to do, I do my best. I've also been known to commit to big projects before I've even figured out how to do them, to work obsessively, to do things quickly and sometimes too fast. And maybe that's why I was at the opposite end, out of gas. Lying in bed that morning, lacking the *oomph* to rise or shine, I thought, *Okay, now what?*

I took a few breaths and observed my thoughts without judgment. Most of my thinking was sliding into the negative end of the pool. Hmmm. One option was to ride the funk out, though, like a week of overcast skies, that could take a while. Or I could be more proactive.

Neuroplasticity is the scientific term for great news: our brains are very pliable, and we can, almost literally, change our minds. Repeated thoughts can embed themselves in our grey matter, much as we can trace a groove in the sand with a finger and make that groove deeper as we trace over and over. Think the same negative thoughts repeatedly, and they become more deeply ingrained, regardless of whether they're rooted in fact. However, this works both ways; thinking positive, supportive, emotionally healthy thoughts repeatedly can create happier, more upbeat thinking. Now *that* could get me out of bed.

The mere thought of it had me pushing off the covers and getting a notebook and pen. I resolved to write three affirmations each morning for the next week. After seven days, I'd see if it made a difference in my mindset.

That week turned into two months. I stopped having trouble getting out of bed early on in the experiment; I kept going for the joy of it. In fact, I couldn't wait to write my affirmations.

What are affirmations, exactly? They're short but powerful statements that create a positive feeling. They affirm our sense of self —our best self, both the good qualities we already possess and the ones we want to cultivate. "Just as we do repetitive physical exercise to get stronger, affirmations can be thought of as exercise for our mind/brain," writes David Schechter, MD, author of The MindBody Workbook on PsychologyToday.com.

There are many affirmations available online, though going online to find them can pull me into rabbit holes of checking email, getting lost on social media, and generally forgetting what I went online to find in the first place. Also, studies show that the more time people spend on social media, the more likely they are to feel isolated and depressed. That is *so* not what we're going for here! I've found it's better to write my own affirmations. That way, they can be tailored to specific goals, moods, and issues I'd like to work with. When we bring knitting into this, it's a powerful combination, the ultimate double-stranded colorwork knit for the mind!

Here's how to get started writing your own affirmations:

1. Use your medKNITation journal, or get a notebook for affirmations, preferably one with an uplifting cover that makes you smile. That way, you'll look forward to seeing this notebook first thing in the morning. Also, have a dedicated pen that will live in your affirmations notebook. (A sparkle

pen? One of those multi-color pens we had as kids? An elegant fountain pen? Again, choose something that makes you smile.) Keep both near your bed, on a nightstand, for easy morning access.

2. When you wake up, before you start thinking about all the things you have to do that day, or all the things you don't want to do, get your affirmations notebook and pen. Write the date, and get ready to write three affirmations.

3. Affirmations are short statements phrased in positive ways. Try to avoid negatively phrased statements such as, "I am not feeling blah." Go for positive phrasing, such as, "I am open-minded," "I am kind," "I am creative."

4. On that note, phrase your affirmations in the first person and the present tense: "I am____" rather than "I want to be the kind of person who ____" or "I wish I ____."

If you'd like, you can write a few affirmations from experts that resonate with you to get you started. I'm no expert, but here's a list of affirmations I've written on my Kindness Hearts. See how you feel as you read them, and write the ones you like in your notebook.

I am a kind and loving person.
I look for the best in everyone.
My smile is my superpower.
My kindness can change someone's day.
I am growing stronger every day.
My body is filled with light and love.
My body is a vessel of love.
My mind is a beautiful, peaceful garden.
My spirit is a river of peace.
I am listening to my intuition more and more.
I see obstacles as opportunities.
I listen to my body and give it what it needs.
I maintain an attitude of gratitude.
I focus on what matters most to me.
I am learning, growing, and evolving every day.

I have a natural sense of peace.

When we first learn to knit or crochet, we have to do it regularly to find our rhythm and build our skills. This is easy because stitching can be fun and soothing at the same time. Using affirmations is similar; while repeating them may seem as strange as learning a new stitch at first, the results feel so good, you'll want to practice regularly.

Next, let's weave your affirmations into your knitting!

AFFIRMATIONS MEDKNITATION

Tools: your meditative project and your medKNITation or affirmations notebook.

Step 1: With your meditative project in hand and your notebook by your side, choose one affirmation to work with, and follow the basic pattern for medKNITation (page 24).

Step 2: For a few moments, let your awareness rest gently on your natural breathing, feeling each inhalation and exhalation.

Step 3: Bring your awareness to your project, engaging your senses, and then begin stitching. Go slowly, finding your rhythm.

Step 4: Begin to incorporate your chosen affirmation into your knitting, reciting it along with your rhythm. Say the affirmation aloud the first few times. There is some evidence that hearing an affirmation in your own voice makes it more resonant. After saying it aloud a few times, even in a whisper, begin to recite it in your mind. Let your affirmation fit your knitting rhythm; you can say part of your affirmation with one stitch, and part for the next.

Continue stitching for however long is comfortable for you. When you're ready to finish, put your project in your lap, close your eyes, and bring your awareness to your breathing. Do three grounding breaths to complete your meditation practice.

A Week of Positivity

We love a knit- or crochet-along, a 30-day challenge, any kind of consistent activity that can make us happier and give us a feeling of accomplishment. This one can change your mindset, as it did mine. Each day for a week, when you wake up, write three affirmations. You can use the ones I gave above, or affirmations from another source, or make up your own. At the end of seven days, review your affirmations and see how you feel. Then, add another week!

23

"TO THINE OWN SELF BE TRUE"
MEDKNITATION

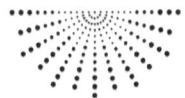

This above all: to thine own self be true,
And it must follow, as the night the day,
Thou canst not then be false to any man.

— POLONIUS TO HIS SON LAERTES IN
HAMLET, ACT I, SCENE 3

When I was young, I was taught a variation on the saying "Honesty is the best policy." My Nana's amendment was, "Unless your friend already got her hair cut, in which case you tell her she looks terrific." Nana's feeling was that when something couldn't be undone at the moment—the hair already cut in an unflattering way, the ill-fitting dress no longer returnable—why make a person feel bad? "Let her think she looks great," Nana said, "and when her hair grows back, tell her she looks even better."

My grandmother's diplomacy showed her compassion for others, along with her practical sensibility. I've had my hair cut short many times, and some well-meaning person has said, "It's too short," or "This look ages you," or "I like it better long." (None of these has come from my husband, a wise man who loves harmony in the home. A few came from my mother, who reserves the right to speak a mother's truth.) These well-meaning comments—unsolicited, mind you—took me from feeling that I looked like a chic Parisian gamine to someone who got the bad-tempered barber at the local chop shop. I can tell myself that person's taste is all in their mouth—another of Nana's sayings—but there's only so comment-proof I can be.

Thankfully, over time, I've come to see this kind of honesty as opinion, not fact. That person didn't like my hair short; this person didn't like one of my books. We sometimes treat other people's opinions as facts, especially depending on the source, though what someone thinks and what's really true are often unrelated.

This is why I find "To thine own self be true" to be a compass pointing toward my own True North. This poetic part of a Shakespearean play turned guiding principle is about sifting through opinions to get to the truth that will, as another saying tells us, set you free. No need for hiding, for betraying yourself, for saying something is okay when it isn't, for saying yes when the answer is no. Never mind what someone else thinks of your hair, your work, your hobby, your life choices; what's in your heart?

Over a period of years, I worked with an online art school. The students are mostly retirees, empty nesters who now have time to do what they want. One of the things they've discovered is that they want to learn how to draw—or, more specifically, learn how to get back to drawing. Many of them have said that, as children, they could draw naturally, and happily, without question. Then, someone came along with an opinion. "That doesn't look like the person you're drawing." "That's not very good." "You can't be an artist." "You don't have any talent." In almost all the cases, the drawing stopped.

Children have a hard time parsing out the difference between facts and opinions, especially when the information is coming from adults they're supposed to listen to and trust. Even if the person was some sort of expert, such as an art teacher, why derail a child's enjoyment? Some of those comments kept people from drawing for many years. Yet the power of "To thine own self be true" can't be denied forever. Despite the damage, these artists' true desire to be creative through drawing was stronger than the opinions that had stopped them years ago. (Interestingly, many of them were knitters as well!)

If drawing or painting or knitting or writing or any creative endeavor was, or is, important, we can't let other people's opinions get in the way of our truth, which is that we want to do these things, sometimes even feel compelled to do them.

Entire books have been written about how people stop us and why we let them. People spend a great deal of time thinking and talking about it. At this point in my life, my preference is to listen to my heart and take action. I don't need other people's opinions to be my beliefs. I have something more powerful: To thine own self be true.

"To Thine Own Self Be True" medKNITation

Tools: your most meditative project.

Note: This meditation requires the simplest of projects, such as a garter stitch scarf. This will help your innermost thoughts swim toward the surface so you can hear them. Give them your loving attention!

Step 1: Follow the basic pattern for medKNITation (page 24).

Step 2: For a few moments, let your awareness rest gently on your natural breathing. Think of your natural breathing pattern as your body's way of expressing truth.

Step 3: Begin knitting. Make the stitches as you normally would, falling gently into your natural stitching rhythm. Feel the yarn moving through your fingers, observe the stitches you're making, and enjoy the process. Let your knitting soothe you and bring you to your natural sense of peace.

Step 4: When you're feeling relaxed, ask yourself if there's something you'd like to do, what activities you may not have done in a while that you'd like to explore again. Let yourself think expansively;

you don't have to do everything that comes up, but some desires may feel stronger than others.

You may encounter some opinions from the past from people who've said "can't" or "shouldn't." Thank them for sharing and move on, letting them be in the same way you'd walk past yarn that doesn't appeal to you.

Return to your gentle inquiry. What might bring you pleasure? What might even be of benefit to others? When we're happy, our happiness can be transmitted to others, so don't be stingy—let yourself think about personal joy.

Continue stitching for however long you like. When you're ready to finish, set your project in your lap, and bring your awareness to your breathing. Do three grounding breaths to complete your meditation practice. Note any discoveries of your truth in your medKNITation journal, and the steps you can take to start making them happen!

Meeting Fear Calmly

Whenever we open up to being true to ourselves, we also encounter obstacles. Sometimes these obstacles are memories of things people have said that stopped us cold. Sometimes it's the fearful part of ourselves trying to keep us from doing something new or thinking bigger. Fear has a place in our lives; it's meant to help keep us safe. It's not meant to keep us from living and trying new things. People sometimes feel anxious during meditation because fears they've pushed down in daily life have a chance to be heard. This is one of the ways medKNITation can be a gentler form of meditation, because having your eyes open and focused on something soft and colorful is soothing and uplifting.

If fear arises during a meditation, be compassionate toward yourself. Try to understand why it's there; is it based on past experience, or is it an opinion someone else told you? Is it about doing something new? Try asking yourself about the fear more than listening to it. Sometimes facing fear, especially when it's unavoidable, reduces it. I try to invite the fear to sit down, have some tea, and tell me why it's there. This gentle approach makes it feel less scary. Remember, your true self is courageous, and the definition of courage is "fear that has said its prayers."

24

ANTIDOTE TO OVERWHELM
MEDKNITATION

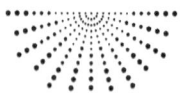

There are people who can juggle dozens of to-dos per day. Medical personnel, politicians, teachers, parents. I'm not a great juggler; I do better when I focus on one thing at a time, because I can very easily become overwhelmed.

I'm not the only one, considering the amount of input we have these days. There seems to be so much going on, everywhere, and we have access to all of it—the twenty-four-hour news cycle, the alerts coming through on our phones. Social media shows us all the things people are doing, including making videos of themselves doing all those things, and it makes us wonder if we should we be doing all of that too. And the email—there's so much email, but how much of it is actually worth our time? I estimate that only thirty percent of the email I get relates in any way to my life. I'd unsubscribe to the others, but that takes up time and attention as well.

A few years ago, I found a wonderful antidote to overwhelm in a book called *Buddhism for Busy People: Finding Happiness in a Hurried World* by David Michie. In a section about how to meditate, Michie's instruction was to bring all your focus to the tip of your nose, observing the sensations of the breath on each inhalation and exhalation. There was more, but that one part spoke to me; focus on one thing. *Ahhh.* This was a way for me to tune out the overwhelm of all the things I had to do and deal with each day for just a few minutes. I could dial down the confusion by bringing all my scattered focus to one point right in front of me.

Hmmm... Sound familiar?

This is what knitting does for us. We can focus all our attention on one thing and give our minds a rest. (It's possible that the entire point of this book is in this one medKNITation, though hopefully you'll like the rest of it, too!) Knitting, crocheting, and stitching bring our focus to one point—one of the key teachings in meditation—and help us quiet the mind so we can find peace.

This is important not only for our own sense of calm. In a *New Yorker* Magazine article called "The Battle for Attention," reporter Nathan Heller wrote that we're losing our ability to focus, and, for young people, at alarming rates. Standard tests for students are being shortened because teenagers and younger children simply can't focus on basic reading assignments. College students are having trouble reading books for the same reason. Scenes in movies and TV shows last mere seconds before cutting to the next scene. Even songs are getting shorter. Our attention spans are being clipped by a bombardment of quick bites of videos, images, and news. All of it adds up to a feeling of overwhelm and, eventually, burnout.

This meditation trains us to build our powers of focus, giving relief from overwhelm. A special note to those who have children in their lives, whether through family, your neighbors, or teaching at school: teaching a child of any age to knit or crochet can help reduce their feelings of overwhelm, too. Pass knit on!

Antidote to Overwhelm medKNITation

Tools: your meditative project.

Step 1: Follow the basic pattern for medKNITation (page 24).
Step 2: Bring your awareness to the tip of your nose. Focus on your breathing by noticing the sensations of each inhalation and

exhalation. The air may feel warmer on the inhalation, slightly cooler on the exhalation.

For a few moments, keep your awareness on these sensations. Let everything else fade to the background as all your focus rests gently on the tip of your nose. Breathing in. Breathing out. Breathing in, and out again. Your thoughts may wander, because your brain has become accustomed to switching from one thought to the next like a social media feed. Gently steer your awareness back to those sensations of inhalation and exhalation.

Step 3: Move your awareness to your stitching. Stitch as you normally would. Notice each motion that goes into making a stitch.

Notice the feeling of the yarn as it moves through your fingers. Notice the sensations in your fingers and hands.

Follow the yarn as it loops through previous loops.

As you did when focusing on the tip of your nose, rest your awareness on the yarn, the movements, the sensations.

Continue stitching for however long you like. When you're ready to finish, set your project in your lap. Bring your awareness to your breathing, feeling the sensations at the tip of your nose again for a few minutes. Notice the gentle power of focus. Do three grounding breaths to complete your meditation.

2 5
TRANSFORMATION
MEDKNITATION

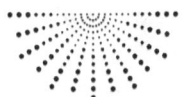

Recently, after I gave a talk about meditating with knitting and crochet, the people who asked me to give the lecture sent feedback from the audience. Of the people who took the time to respond, ninety-nine percent loved the lecture, saying the meditations made them feel calmer and that they wanted to keep medKNITating on their own. Some of them asked the event hosts to have me back for more sessions of meditation with knitting.

Then there was one person who didn't like it. When I say she didn't like it, she really didn't like it, and she did not hold back in her not-liking. There was nothing specific in her feedback that I could learn from—or so I thought.

I'd love to say I shrugged it off and went about my life. After all, I meditate, and write books and give lectures about meditation and mindfulness; surely, I just float above criticism, maybe even express gratitude for it. Um...no. Hopefully it won't surprise you to learn that the reason I practice meditation and mindfulness in the first place is because things like this can really get to me.

Knitting creates a rich space for contemplation. You sit and make repetitive motions that calm the mind, you hold soft yarn in colors you love... Knitting has the capacity to do something increasingly remarkable in this fast-paced era, which is to give us time and space to think, to consider, to be in a relaxed frame of mind in which we may be able to see things differently. Having the time and space for contemplation can transform experiences that initially seemed negative into something useful. I think of it in the same way that repurposing yarn transforms material that's old or worn out into a meaningful, helpful object.

Years ago, I'd found a type of yarn blended with cheery colors—pink, orange, yellow, lavender. It was smooshy and delightful, and I bought bags of it with the intention of making a throw. I happily crocheted granny squares, and then, less happily, seamed them all together. My husband and I loved the throw, and so did our cats, and we all used it for cozying up on weekends and cat naps.

The yarn didn't wear well; after a while, it frayed and pilled and generally looked like it had been through a lot. A kind description would be that it was "well loved." I couldn't keep it on the couch anymore (time to get more yarn for a new throw!), but what would I do with this throw, or, even if I unraveled it, all the now-worn yarn? The thought came quickly: cat beds! I undid the throw and transformed the material into two cat beds, one for Norman and the other for Sherman, the rescue kitty we'd just adopted. I had fun crocheting, nothing was wasted, and the cats were thrilled with the results.

Like the yarn that initially looked ready for the rubbish bin but was actually perfect for another purpose, I think experiences that initially seem sour can also be transformed into something good, provided we create the time and space for that transformation to occur. When I got that criticism about my lecture, sure, I felt stung. Instead of focusing on my hurt feelings (which is just the ego complaining, and which also feeds the hurt), I took the advice of Buddhist nun and teacher Pema Chödrön and thought about how we're all connected. Other people's feelings get hurt by criticism too. Had I criticized people in the past? Uh, yeah. When I was a music journalist, criticism was actually part of my job. We writers sometimes tried to outdo each other with clever critiques of the albums people had worked hard to make, not thinking about how those wittily barbed reviews might make the musicians feel when they read them.

That was in the days of print magazines, which had a limited reach. What about now, when the internet can reach so many more people? I recently watched a music video by a band that was proudly unveiling their first new song in years. While some fans loved the song and the video, there were many who didn't, and they didn't sugarcoat their comments. These were not variations on "Well, you've done better in the past, but good on ya for rocking on!" The comments were downright hostile (and these were from alleged fans of the band). Such hostility isn't reserved for the music world, either. We've seen it happen everywhere, even in the knitting community.

There's nothing inherently wrong with reviews. The person who didn't like my lecture was being asked to give her opinion because the people who run the lecture series want to keep the standards of their presentations high. Whenever I order a new product, I read reviews by people who are sharing information I might need, like that the yarn is a pleasure to work with or that it won't survive a series of catnaps. What I question is why people have to be mean in expressing their opinions, and even seem to enjoy being mean.

Though I'd initially thought there was nothing of value in the mean critique I'd gotten about my lecture, sitting with it in the transformative space of turning the worn-out throw into the kitty beds gave me a different perspective—not about my lecture, but about criticism. The experience was transformed into a teaching moment. The next time I had an opportunity to voice an opinion about something, especially online, where potentially thousands of people might read it, I would pause—wow, the power of the pause. I can't say enough good things about pausing, which people rarely do in this immediate culture. During a pause for a few breaths or a few rows of knitting, I remember the guidance of Bernard Meltzer, the host of a call-in radio show called "What's Your Problem?", who said:

Before you speak, ask yourself if what you are going to say is true, is kind, is necessary, is helpful. If the answer is no, maybe what you are about to say should be left unsaid.

Bernard Meltzer also said, "The good people in the world far outnumber the bad." I would like to be counted among the good.

During my Yoga teacher training, my teachers spoke about how our energy can affect others. The physical practice of Yoga concerns energy—the energy of the person doing Yoga, the energy of the person teaching, the energy of the group in the class. One of the reasons people like Yoga is that the teacher, the people, and the environment are calming and uplifting. Yoga philosophy also concerns energy, the energy of the actions we take in our daily lives: What are we putting out into the world? Anyone, not just people who do Yoga, can contemplate that. With each action, we can ask: Am I putting out the bad energy of judgment, disdain, even hatred? Or am I being, as Bernard Meltzer said, one of the good people?

There's another saying I always remember: Hurt people hurt people. That may be true, but I'd also like to think that hurt people *help* people. We've all had the experience of being hurt, and we remember how it feels. We also all have the power to transform material, whether yarn or the stuff of our lives, from something bad into something good. When we do that, we go from hurting to healing. We heal ourselves, and we can heal others, too.

There will be times when something hurts my feelings, as that review of my lecture did. Now, instead of feeling hurt and lashing out at the person who hurt me, or at someone else, I can transform that energy into something good. I have a game I play where, if I get a negative comment online, I post five positive comments on other people's feeds. Transformative, I tell you—try it!

There are times when I'll be presented with an opportunity to give an opinion about something. I'm grateful that knitting gives me a way to create space and capacity for contemplation—the power of the pause. With these excellent tools, I can transform negative experiences into something good, and then I can share that good energy.

TRANSFORMATION med**KNIT**tation

Tools: a project you want to unravel and repurpose. You can also use your powers of visualization. This is an especially helpful meditation to do if you've been on the receiving end of some criticism.

Step 1: Sit comfortably, with either your project in hand or your hands folded in your lap. Let yourself tune into your breathing, following your inhalations and exhalations.

Take three deep breaths, imagining with each breath that you're clearing your mind of anything that isn't useful, knowing that your breaths are repurposed into helpful air for plants. After the three deep, cleansing breaths, return to your natural breathing pattern.

Step 2: If you're working with a project you'd like to unravel, begin by acknowledging the project's time in this form, and that it's time to transform it into something else. (This step helps to cultivate respect for others, and for the material items in our lives, and the respect helps us find a way to transform our experiences and materials.) If you're using your imagination, bring to mind a project you've unraveled in the past, or an old sweater that's come to the end of its rainbow, so to speak. Find an end and begin to unravel your project.

Step 3: Whether working with a physical project or visualizing, imagine transforming this yarn into something useful. Let your mind be spacious with possibilities of what you could create.

As you unravel the project, be aware that you're strengthening your powers of contemplation. Within contemplation, the seeds for options and ideas burst open, take root, and grow. Feel yourself relaxing and becoming aware of the different ways this material, whether yarn or experience, is rich with possibilities. You have the power to transform it into something of benefit, both to yourself and to others—even if that benefit is coming to the decision to release the material.

If you're working with a physical project, unravel as much as you want to, winding your yarn into neat balls as you go along. If you're using your imagination, visualize unraveling your project, then winding your yarn into a neat ball.

When you're ready to finish, set your project aside, close your eyes, and let your awareness rest on your breathing as you feel the satisfaction of having transformed your material, and your experience. Know that you've built your powers of contemplation and can now pause before reacting. This is like a muscle, and the more you use it, the more discerning you can be in how you share your energy. You can transform pain into kindness. You have that superpower.

Conclude your meditation with three grounding breaths.

26

SOFT AND STRONG
MEDKNITATION

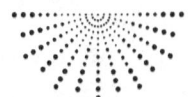

One of the most appealing things about yarn is its softness. From the time we're babies, the feeling of being wrapped in something soft and warm is instantly comforting. We don't lose that feeling when we get bigger and older. We may need it just as much, which is why there are patterns for oversized sweaters made of thick, plushy yarn, and large blankets and throws that always have a starring role in the fantasy of curling up with a good book and a cup of tea.

For something so soft, though, yarn can be very strong. Some yarn will fall apart at the slightest tug, but for the most part, yarn can be a lot stronger than it looks.

One day, before a meditation, I was holding a ball of baby pink yarn. This fuzzy ball was so adorable, and the color invoked such images of cuteness, that if I'd put a pair of googly eyes on it, I could've turned it into a pet. (No feeding or litter box required!) Yet I knew from having worked with this yarn that it wasn't nearly as delicate as it looked. This yarn would *endure*.

I remember watching a show where two people were debating a political topic. One person shouted, yelled, was absolutely vehement about their feelings. The other person spoke using a normal tone of voice, presented facts rather than opinions, and remained composed and unruffled. That person came across as being far more reasonable than the louder counterpart, who became even more apoplectic due to the calm person's refusal to engage in the shouting match. Similarly, I used to work with a woman who spoke quietly but directly. In conference rooms full of men battling to get their points across, when this woman spoke, everyone paused to hear what she was saying.

In recent times, a culture of being loud and in-your-face is presented as strength—usually by the people who are yelling. Any knitter can tell you that softness doesn't automatically equate to weakness. Entire nations have changed from harsh political regimes to ones based on fairness through the non-violent work of people like Mahatma Gandhi and Nelson Mandela. These leaders may have seemed to take a gentle stance, but their wills were stronger than steel. Closer to home, I have a friend who told me recently, "I haven't found the need to yell at anyone in twenty years." As this person is no pushover and does not put up with nonsense, I expressed disbelief that she hadn't been aggravated in two decades. My friend shook her head. "I get aggravated all the time, but if I yell, the message gets lost in the delivery," she said. "Whatever I have to say, I say it, kindly if I can, directly if the person gives me pushback. But I don't yell, because that disturbs *my* peace."

By the way, this person is a knitter. She makes the softest, prettiest shawls while taking zero crap from anyone.

Maybe using yarn as a metaphor for the point that softness can be strong is a stretch (and I've managed to throw a bad pun in here as well). Yet in this time of division, maybe a simple metaphor is all we need to bring us back to the time when we were children, wrapped in warm cozy blankets made of soft yarn that would endure long enough to be given to those children's children, and we were unaware of any differences between us.

Soft and Strong medKNITation

Tools: a soft ball, skein, or hank of yarn. You can also wrap yourself in a cozy shawl or throw.

Step 1: Holding your yarn in your hands, or wrapping yourself in your shawl or blanket, follow the basic pattern for medKNITation (page 24).

Step 2: For a few moments, let your awareness rest gently on your natural breathing. If you'd like, remember a time in your childhood when you were wrapped in something soft, such as a blanket, a towel, a quilt. Bring that feeling of warmth and safety to mind as you breathe.

Step 3: You can keep your eyes closed or open as you feel a strand of your yarn. Notice the softness of the fibers, the fuzziness, the way the yarn feels in your fingers and hands. You can stroke your cheek with the yarn if you want to and smoosh it in your hands.

Now give the yarn strand a pull. Feel that the yarn is strong, maybe stronger than it looks.

Let the feeling of softness and strength fill your fingers, your hands, your arms, all the way into the rest of your body.

With either hand, lightly touch your opposite arm. Feel the softness of your skin. Know that there is great strength within you. Know that you can be stronger than you think.

Holding your yarn, say silently to yourself, *I am soft and strong.*

When you're ready to finish your meditation, bring your awareness back to your breathing, which is also soft and strong. Then, do three grounding breaths to complete your meditation.

27

WINDING TO UNWIND
MEDKNITATION

"Would you like me to wind the yarn for you?" the kind person at the yarn shop asked.

"No thanks," I said. "I'll wind it myself."

The look the person at the counter gave me was a combination of surprise and "suit yourself." I couldn't blame her, given that I'd just bought three bundles of fingering-weight yarn. Not the chunky stuff that could be wound quickly and easily; this was the thin kind where the only easy part is tangling it up.

Granted, I was a new knitter at the time, yet I've repeated this conversation during more than a few yarn shop visits since then. (The look that follows is always the same.) Most people—mindful of time, wanting to dive into their project, sane—choose to have their new yarn fitted onto a winder and watch it get spun into neat cakes while they wait. There's something very meditative about that. Some even get their own winders so they can do it themselves.

I have no winder at home (other than my husband, whose sense of orderliness gravitates toward projects such as winding yarn). When I was new to yarn and didn't know that winding by hand takes a long time and is full of potential for tangling, I foolishly decided to wind my own.

In Tarot cards, the first card in the major arcana is The Fool. People who get this card usually think it means they're being foolish or gullible or some variation on none too smart, but that's not the card's true meaning. The person in the card represents innocence. To them, everything is new, a fresh experience. The card is also the first in the Major Arcana of Tarot, signifying a new beginning.

The Fool carries only a small bag of past experience, setting out seemingly unaware of being on the edge of a cliff. Yet it's through the Fool's openness to new experiences that the path is formed, each step revealing itself as the person goes along.

Maybe the way things are usually done isn't always the way we have to do them. Yes, most people get their yarn wound at the shop, but when I was new to knitting—an innocent Fool happily going off on this fresh adventure—I thought I'd try something different.

When I got my new yarn home, I saw why people choose to have their yarn wound at the shop. Yikes; so many thin strands, so much potential for a big tangle of yarn spaghetti. I thought I should hang it from something as I wound it, so I looped it over a doorknob. (My husband wasn't home at the time, or his hands would've been my first choice.) I found an end and began wrapping the soft yarn around my fingers, then around the small ball that was forming.

Winding yarn, even carefully, doesn't require much attention, so my mind had a chance to wander, much like the Fool going off in an unspecified direction. Recent conversations drifted into my mind like a breeze through an open window, then drifted away. Things I had to do appeared and vanished. Gradually, my mind settled into an openness; the solid ground of rigid thinking disappeared, and a new path formed with each moment. Ideas flirted. Questions formed, not needing an answer right in that moment. As I wound the yarn, I unwound my usual need-to-know thinking.

I'll be the first to admit I was a little hasty when I refused winding for three skeins of yarn; that was too much meditation even for me! But every now and then, when I have one skein or hank that needs to be wound into a ball, I sit down and settle in for what I know will be a relaxing meditation.

WINDING TO UNWIND medKNITATION

Tools: a hank or skein of yarn.

For this meditation, the most important step comes before you start: make sure you're comfortable. Winding yarn can take a while, especially if you don't want to end up with a hopelessly tangled mess. I've sat on a cushion or a pile of blankets on the floor and hung the yarn on a doorknob, and when I need to stand for a while, I've used a coat hook. Alternate between sitting and standing wherever you can hang your yarn and work comfortably.

Step 1: Begin with three grounding breaths, and then allow your awareness to rest on your body's natural breathing pattern for a few moments.

Step 2: Engage your senses by looking at your yarn; touching it and smooshing it; sniffing it to see if it has any sort of scent.

Step 3: Hang your yarn on your preferred doorknob, coat hook, or whatever you're using. Find an end and begin winding. Take your time, going at a comfortable pace, not too fast or slow. Observe your movements for a moment or two. Your mind will begin to drift. Let it go where it wants to go. The repetitive motion will naturally lead to a meditative state. Just observe, without judgment, wherever you go as you wind. Be like The Fool, open to the journey.

Continue winding until you're finished, or for however long is comfortable for you. When you're ready, set your freshly wound yarn in your lap. Close your eyes, bring your awareness to your breathing, and do three grounding breaths to complete your meditation practice. Make note of any adventures in thinking you had in your notebook.

28

GOING INWARD MEDKNITATION

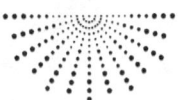

When I was a teenager, I went to art school to study cartooning. My plan was to follow in my biological father's footsteps. Art school and I didn't get along, though, and at that point, neither did my father and I. All of us parted ways for some time, and I had to choose a new direction for what might be the rest of my life. (Years later, my father and I would bond happily over our mutual love of drawing, and of life itself. How things can change, if we let them!)

I didn't know what to do. My mother wisely saw that I needed skills beyond being able to draw a caricature of myself, so she sent me to secretarial school. Anyone remember what that was? You learned how to type really fast and take shorthand. Anyone remember what *that* was?

Both in art school and in secretarial school, I excelled in English classes. I loved to read and write. I studied short stories, novels, nonfiction, memoir, and poetry, and books were among my best friends. I never thought about becoming a writer, though; that felt like something bestowed upon the talented, privileged few, like people who are born into royalty.

For a while, I did secretarial work, answering phones and typing business letters, and then I was accepted to a university. My major was

Media Studies, with a minor in Art History, and as usual, I did great in my English classes. I read, I wrote, I fell in love with words, and I still had no idea what to do with my life.

Summer came, school was out, and my mother gently but firmly informed me that I couldn't just hang around the house; I needed to get a job or an internship. The latter sounded more interesting, and I called my favorite pop music magazine, the one with Duran Duran and Billy Idol on its covers, and asked if they needed a summer intern. Sorry, they said, we already have our interns. Oh, I said. Then I asked, "Do any of those interns type 90 words per minute?" They told me to come down that afternoon for an interview.

Somehow, my love of reading, writing, and that Mom-mandated stint in secretarial school merged to form my career in writing for magazines. I became a pop music journalist, then a celebrity journalist, then an essayist, and an editor along the way. I'd found what I wanted to do for the rest of my life.

In 2008, an economic crisis met a surge in media on the internet. The result was the thinning out of print media. Most of the magazines I'm proud to have written for have folded. Some people have never even heard of them. When I realized my job as a magazine writer and editor was the modern equivalent of a horse-and-buggy driver when cars began to rule the road, I had to go forward. But, I thought, I'm a magazine writer. Where do I go from here?

To many places, as it turned out. Since my last magazine job in 2008, I've written books, I've taught Yoga and meditation, I've led classes in writing, and I've taught meditation through knitting and art. My career path has had many off ramps, twists, turns, the occasional scenic view and photo opportunity—so many that I couldn't go by one title, or call myself one thing. A person can't be defined by a title, an occupation, or their circumstances.

A friend who lived in Europe for a while had an interesting observation: in conversations, the first question Americans ask someone they've just met is "What do you do?", while Europeans will talk about everything else—how you know the people who introduced you, where you're from, what it's like there, the food you're all eating... They may never get around to asking you what you do for work. It's not that they don't care, they just don't think about people as being defined by their occupation.

Since I stopped defining myself by a job title, I've been able to explore who I am as a person. Without the constraints of definition by something outside of myself, usually something I can't control, I can grow, evolve, and become more and more comfortable in my own being. This has been especially valuable, even essential, as I get older.

We can refuse the easy packaging of being defined by our circumstances, whether it's a job, a life stage, an illness. For example, I use the phrase, "S/he is working with cancer" rather than "S/he is a cancer patient" because people who are experiencing illnesses or conditions don't like being defined by that one part of their lives. My friend Francesco is not a "quadriplegic," he's a person—a husband, father, son, brother, uncle, friend, the head of a skincare line... The fact that he happens to be in a wheelchair isn't the most interesting part of his life. Why be penned in by a concept when you're so much more, and have so much more yet to be?

The way forward, I've learned, is the way inward. I don't want to be defined by something outside of myself; I want to explore the terrain of my own heart and boundless mind. There are many ways to do this, which has led me to one small exception of my "no titles" rule: I will happily say that I am a knitter and crocheter. For me, those descriptions are synonymous with being a seeker of truth.

GOING INWARD medKNITATION

Tools: a ball of yarn, and whatever size knitting needles or crochet hook work with that yarn.

In some cases, we have to go forward because a part of life has changed, and other times, we're just ready for a fresh new beginning. The choice to go forward may have been ours, or it was made for us. Even when it's the latter, we still have a choice to take that first step forward by going inward, exploring the occasionally rugged, always beautiful terrain of who we truly are. This meditation can help you take that first step on your path.

Step 1: Take your yarn and needles or hook in hand. Today, think of them as the tools that will facilitate this next part of your journey.

Step 2: Follow the basic pattern for medKNITation (page 24). For a few moments, let your awareness rest gently on your natural breathing pattern. Think of each breath as a new beginning, a fresh step on a lush, vibrant road of possibilities.

Step 3: Cast on enough stitches for a scarf. Though you may have been making the motions that create stitches for so long that they're automatic, slow down, noticing each motion.

Think of each stitch as another step along your path. Where will you go from here? You don't have to think too much about it. See the orderliness of your stitches as you begin to knit or crochet. Keep the stitches simple, stockinette or an easy crochet stitch, just as you would like to keep the steps going forward simple.

Let your mind be soothed by the repetitive motions of your stitches. Let yourself think expansively. You are not defined by a title, status, condition, anything. How could you possibly be defined by those things? You are limitless!

Again, there's no need to think too hard about this. Let go of effort and let your mind drift, soothed by the creation of each new stitch, each new step within, each new breath.

Continue stitching for however long you like. When you're ready to finish, set your project in your lap, close your eyes, and bring your awareness to your breathing. Do three grounding breaths to complete your meditation practice—and open your eyes to your new beginning.

29
CONNECTION MEDKNITATION

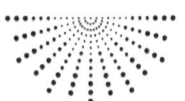

At the end of each meditation session, there's a transition from the meditative space, the inward experience, and back into the "real" world, the present moment. It's a bridge best crossed slowly and gently. My teachers led us to it through awareness of the breath, then feeling sensations in the body, slowly opening the eyes, and then enjoying a nice stretch as we rejoined the world.

The word Yoga means "union," and that can be interpreted as the union of body and breath, of body, mind, and spirit, of a person and their Higher Power. In knitting, one stitch is united, or connected, with the ones next to it. In medKNITation, when I offered the idea that each breath could be seen as a stitch, one leading into the next, people understood instantly.

When I sat with that large group of knitters at Vogue Knitting Live and led them through medKNITation, I thought about how wonderful it is that knitting can bring together a room full of people from different places, many of whom probably had different ideas, beliefs, opinions. Yet there we all were, sitting together, knitting together, breathing together. This beautiful vision of peaceful people made me see how, despite some differences, we're all connected.

People have had differences since time began, and we've also had great capacity for connection. Even if we don't agree with someone else, we can listen, and we can respect their personal experiences (mostly unknown to us, unless we ask). Connection is vital to us, for our physical survival, but also for our emotional health.

Knitting has given me and other people I know a chance to connect with others. I've shared the story of how I went to Knitty City to take knitting lessons and ended up making many friends, some of whom I know I'll be connected to for life. Others have had similar experiences. Even if people can't get out much due to health issues or living in remote areas, we can connect with other stitchers through online groups.

Without connection, knitting doesn't happen. If those stitches don't stick together, you have a pile of little pieces of yarn. Same with us; if we don't see that we're all connected, we go to pieces.

At the end of each meditation session I lead, in that moment when we go from our individual, inward experience to rejoining the room and seeing other people, I ask the participants to extend their arms out to their sides. I call it a nice stretch, and then I tell people that by doing this, we're all connecting with each other. This is especially resonant during online sessions. We may seem to be alone in our spaces, but in reality, we're like stitches, all connected.

Connection med**KNIT**ation

Tools: your meditative project.

Step 1: Find your comfortable seat. Have your meditation project in your lap. Begin with a breathing meditation: take three grounding breaths, then let your body breathe the way it wants to breathe. Let your awareness rest on your inhalations and your exhalations. Imagine your breaths as being like stitches, one connected to the next.

Know that everyone breathes in the same way, and that we're all breathing together, all connected by the breath.

Step 2: Follow the basic pattern for medKNITation (page 24).

Step 3: Begin stitching. Notice how each stitch is connected to the one before it, the one after it, and all the other stitches.

Consider how we're connected with other people—our families, our friends, the people we come into contact with each day. Each of us breathing together, one breath into the next.

We may have differences, and we also have similarities. We're all connected, like the stitches in our knitting.

We don't always have to agree with everyone, we don't even have to like everyone, but we can let each person breathe and be, and be connected to them. As knitters, we know the power and value of connection. We honor our connection with each stitch, each breath.

Continue stitching for however long you like. When you're ready to finish, set your project in your lap, close your eyes, and bring your awareness to your breathing. Do three grounding breaths to complete your meditation practice. As you open your eyes, extend your arms outward for a nice stretch, and as a way to connect with everyone.

30

WEAVERS OF OUR LIVES
MEDKNITATION

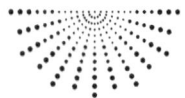

When I went back to knitting after some time away due to caregiving and a few all-consuming jobs, I wanted to re-create my first wonderful knitting experience, learning from a teacher in a cozy, colorful yarn shop. I found Knitty City on the upper west side of Manhattan and signed up for a beginner's class. Within an hour, Maxine Levinson became my knitting guru, taking me through re-learning by knitting a scarf. In subsequent lessons, we went on to arm warmers and a lovely, ribbed cowl. At each lesson, other beginner students and I sat at one of Knitty City's tables elbow-to-elbow with expert knitters making intricate shawls. Fast friendships were made at those tables.

With each project Maxine took me through, I began to feel like I had the potential to become a real knitter, someone who could take two sticks and a ball of yarn, or, later, a hook and yarn, and weave beautiful, useable things out of thin air. Each time I sat at that table and watched someone make a sweater, I thought, *That could be me some day!* This was an empowering feeling. For me, the yarn shop was a place filled with potential.

Many people have written about the phenomenon of the yarn stash, including the wonderful essayists in Clara Parkes's *A Stash of One's Own: Knitters on Loving, Living With, and Letting Go of Yarn*. One of the theories put forth by people who consider the reasons for vast, space- and cat-engulfing yarn stashes is something I felt in the yarn shop during my beginner's classes: potential.

A ball, hank, or skein of yarn symbolizes possibility—possibility that requires us to make it happen. The yarn is like a cocoon: What kind of butterfly could be made from this? That process happens by nature's magic. For something to be made from yarn and sticks, we're the necessary catalyst. That's also magic. We see yarn, we imagine possibility, and we know this thing we want to make isn't going to happen with luck or hope or wishing. It happens when we make it happen. Potential, meet Agency. A perfect match.

On the surface, you could say that people buy lots of yarn because they might not see a certain type again. Independent dyers make small batches, yarn goes on sale—there are many practical reasons. The magical reason I've bought yarn without having a specific pattern or idea of what I'll make out of it is potential. Not the yarn's potential; my own.

Why do so many of us start fitness programs, vow to quit smoking, swear we'll start meditating, and make other self-improvement promises on January 1? Because a fresh new year is full of potential for positive change. You could start these beneficial habits on any date, but the first day of January has that "new year" smell.

When it comes to yarn, though, there's no need to wait for the start of a new year. (Wait? LOL!) New yarn signals potential the moment you hold it in your hand. Like a mythical instrument, it bestows upon the bearer the title of Maker. You, with your two hands and two magic wands, or even one, can transform this material into something special.

We have other instruments of potential in our lives. Car keys have the potential to get you wherever you want to go, and your phone is an entire digital universe, for better or worse. Those objects, important as they may be, involve a less intimate transaction. Yes, it's empowering to be a driver, and it's great to be able to look up anything on your phone, but when I'm scrolling mindlessly, I have to ask myself: What have I done with all that potential of time?

Yarn allows us to create. Yarn gives us the potential to make something necessary, something frivolous and fun, an item that will be loved for generations or worn to pieces in a single season. Yarn says: You decide. You can do whatever you want. If you don't know how to make it now, you can learn.

The potential imbued in yarn is an apt metaphor for our own potential. When something we're weaving isn't going well, we can unravel it and change directions. We can do the same thing in our lives. We can restart our days. We can reinvent ourselves. Think about it: *We are the weavers of our own lives.*

When yarn calls to me (and if you work with fiber, you know yarn calls to you!), when it sings its song of what it can be, I see visions of myself wearing something I made out of this material. The person wearing that handmade garment in my vision is also someone I made. Yes, I think, I can be that person: someone who wove that shawl, someone who follows her own internal rhythm. A friend of mine once said, "I feel like I've come into myself." That's what potential means to me, and what yarn symbolizes so well. When I hold yarn, I envision what it could be, and I know I can make that vision real.

If I can do that...what else can I do?

To me, yarn holds not only the potential for hours of meditative making and, ultimately, a hand-made garment, but my own potential. I can be the kind of person I see in my mind's vision of my best self.

WEAVERS OF OUR LIVES medKNITation

Tools: any yarn you're about to use or would like to use, whether it's brand new or something you've brought out from the depths of your stash.

A powerful figure in Native American traditions is Spider-Woman, who wove a map of the universe. She is considered the loving force behind sacred weaving. I like to keep her in mind whenever I knit to this meditation.

Step 1: Follow the basic pattern for medKNITation (page 24).

Step 2: Hold your ball, skein, or hank of yarn. Take a moment to admire the colors and the way the fibers are woven together. Feel the texture with your fingers and hands, then bring the yarn up to your face and feel it. Smoosh the yarn, which is resilient and bounces back. Then relax your arms and let your hands, holding the yarn, rest in your lap.

Step 3: Close your eyes. Allow the idea of potential to blossom in your mind. Think of the yarn's potential, about what you'd like to make with it.

Think of your own potential. What you'd like to become.

With the power of your own consciousness, you can create. You can change, and help create positive change.

You can become anything you want. The yarn is symbolic of your own potential.

Step 4: Consider what you would like to do and where you want to focus your energies. You can also bring these to mind while you're knitting or crocheting with the yarn.

Aloud or silently, repeat the mantra: *I am the weaver of my life.*

When you're ready to finish, bring your awareness to your breathing for a moment or two. Then do three grounding breaths to complete your practice. Write down your thoughts on your potential in your medKNITation book. Do this meditation a few times a month, or as needed, to keep strengthening that vision of your best self.

PART III
YOGA FOR YARN LOVERS

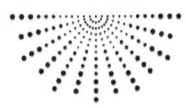

YOGA FOR YARN LOVERS

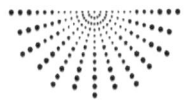

Knitting means sitting, and the more we love to knit, the more we sit. Meditation also usually means sitting, and now, we're combining both. This is wonderful for our minds, and, in this section, we're going to learn how to take care of our bodies, because the fact is, sitting for too long isn't too good for our health. The increasingly sedentary nature of our lives—sitting in front of computers, in cars, while we binge-watch TV while knitting, can actually cause quite a bit of damage to our beautiful physical selves. A report from Yale Medicine stated that prolonged sitting has been linked to weight gain, depression, heart issues, and even diabetes and some forms of cancer. Yikes!

Fortunately, it's easy enough to counteract this potential damage. As a longtime Yoga practitioner and instructor, I know how adaptable and gentle Yoga can be, and I've modified a series of Yoga-inspired movements and poses specifically for stitchers. Welcome to Yoga for Yarn Lovers!

You don't have to know anything about Yoga to do these movements, you don't have to be physically fit, a certain body type, or own a Yoga mat. These movements are suitable for almost any body. And, because your amazing body has infinite wisdom, I encourage you to **do only what feels good to *you*.** For example, if there's an instruction here to raise your arms, and you have shoulder issues that mean you can raise your arms only to a certain point comfortably, just do that. Listening to your body is a form of meditation and an act of self-care. All the instructions for these movements are offerings, not set-in-stone musts. Remember: Do what feels right for *you*.

When I'm doing a medKNITation, I don't have to worry about moving because I'm only sitting for ten to fifteen minutes. When I'm knitting in the evening and my husband and I are sitting through a movie or a few episodes of a show, I get up every twenty to thirty minutes for a few movements (and maybe a walk to the kitchen for more water and a snack). That's my practice, and my suggestion: **Every twenty to thirty minutes, or every five rows of a shawl or blanket, stand up and move around.** A few tips:

- **Set a timer.** When I'm working on a project, I get so meditative I can lose track of time. Set a timer on your phone, or, if you're watching a show, get up at every commercial.
- **Keep this book in your project bag.** That way, you can choose which movements you want to do, and do different ones every time.
- **Remember that it feels good!** You know how a nice stretch feels in the morning? These movements are like that. When you sit too long, you can feel stiff when you finally stand. These movements will keep you from feeling creaky when you get up.
- **In a wheelchair? No worries.** You can do a lot with arm movements and, if your range of motion permits, simple twists. Remember to massage your legs to aid your circulation. Even if you can't feel it, your body knows you're doing it and will get the benefits!

To do these movements, read through the instructions first, and then do them yourself. These gentle stretches should feel good, and again, if something doesn't feel good, don't do it. There are suggestions for other kinds of movement at the end of this section.

HEEL LIFTS

After you've been sitting for a while, ease into movement with this warm-up. Start by standing with your feet hip width apart, and place your hands on your hips. You can also steady yourself with one hand on the back of a chair. Lift the heel of your right foot, as though you were trying on a high-heeled shoe, then bring that heel down. Lift the heel of your left foot, coming to the ball of that foot, then bring that heel down. Alternate for a few times to flex your feet. Then bring both heels to the floor and wiggle your toes.

SHOULDER ROLLS

Next, stand with your feet hip width apart, feet flat on the floor. Let your arms be relaxed and loose at your sides. Gently roll your shoulders up toward your ears, then back and down. Your shoulders don't have to come close to your ears, just toward them (no straining!).

KNEE CIRCLES

If you have knee issues, you can skip this one. If not, stand with feet hip width apart and place your hands on your hips. Lean on your right leg without putting your hip out. Lift your left heel, keeping the ball of your foot on the floor, and make small, slow circles with your knee. Place your foot flat on the floor and change to do the other leg.

HULA HIPS

Stand with feet hip width apart and bring your hands to your hips. Starting toward the right, make slow, gentle circles with your hips, five circles total. You don't have to go too far out! Then do the same going in the opposite direction, toward the left, making five circles total.

HANK STRETCH

This is fun to do when you have a hank of yarn you have yet to wind. Stand with your feet hip width apart. (You can also do this seated.) Place your hands inside your hank of yarn and spread them apart, as though you were holding it for someone to wind. Raise your arms overhead, or, if you have shoulder concerns, put your arms out in front of you and keep your elbows bent. Lean to the right (not too far). Come back to center. Lean to the left. Come back to center. Repeat a few times, feeling a nice stretch in your side ribs and, if your arms are raised, in your shoulders.

SELF-HUG STRETCH

We've heard that hugs are good for us, but did you know that hugging yourself can also soothe pain, improve your mood, *and* give your back and arms a nice stretch? It's true, and it feels lovely! Get bonus benefits by incorporating your breath with the movements. Start by standing with feet hip width apart. Inhale a comfortably deep breath as you spread your arms out to the sides. As you exhale, wrap your arms around yourself, bring your chin toward your chest, and think kind thoughts for yourself. Repeat a few times for a few more hugs!

YARN FROM HEAVEN STRETCH

This is a nice stretch for arms, shoulders, and sides. You can modify the movements by raising your arms only as far as is comfortable. Stand with your feet hip width apart. Pretend there's beautiful yarn above you (or, if modifying, on a shelf). Reach with first your right arm, grasp the imaginary yarn to give your fingers and hand muscles a stretch, and then bring your arm down slowly. Then reach up with your left arm, grasp with your fingers, and bring your arm down slowly. Repeat three more times, alternating arms.

STANDING AND SEATED TWIST

Give your back a gift with a gentle twist. Only go as far as is comfortable for you. (If you have back issues, or if you're pregnant, please skip this one.) If standing, stand with feet hip width apart. If seated, lengthen your torso as far as is comfortable. Place your hands on your hips. Keeping feet and hips forward, turn toward the right. You don't have to go too far to get a nice stretch. Come back to center mindfully, turn toward the left, and come back to center. Repeat twice.

MORE MOVEMENT

Here are some simple things I do to bring more movement into my knitting time:

- **Standing Cast On:** Each time you cast on for a new project, stand, rather than sitting.
- **Drink water:** When I tell this to people, they say, "But then I'll have to go to the bathroom more." Exactly! Not only does drinking water keep you hydrated, you'll get a walk from the couch to the bathroom. Even if it's not far, it counts as movement.
- **Pretend you don't have a remote:** Back in the day, we had to get up to change the TV channel. These days, you can't even do that manually—but you can pretend. When you want to change the channel, get up with the remote and go over to the TV.
- **Dance:** I'm a big fan of a quick little happy dance. Have a playlist of your favorite songs on your phone. Every half hour or do, dance to a song, or just do a little shimmy.
- **Show your hands some love:** Our most valuable tools are our hands and fingers, which do a lot of work for us in knitting. Show them some appreciation by massaging each hand, finger, and wrist. As always, this should feel good. Start gently and experiment with pressure. Bonus points if you do this while standing and shifting from foot to foot!

We want to knit happily and healthfully for as long as we can. By taking just a few minutes at intervals to stretch and move around, we're giving ourselves the gift of honoring our miraculous bodies, which do so much for us. A healthy knitter is a happy knitter. I wish you much health, happiness, and knitting!

THE KINDNESS HEARTS PROJECT

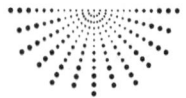

We can focus on everything that's wrong in the world, or we can put our precious life energy toward building and strengthening the good. I like to take action through kindness.

I started the Kindness Hearts Project in 2019 as a way to lift people's spirits, remind them of their essential goodness, and encourage people to share more kindness. The project was simple: make little crocheted or knitted hearts, attach a kind message to them, and put them out into the world.

My early efforts didn't have the world-changing results I'd hoped for, because my delivery method was faulty: I was leaving the hearts in public places for them to be found and taken. Weeks would go by, and I'd see the hearts hanging in the same places I'd left them. Clearly, this wasn't working.

As I shared with you in the introduction, I had the wonderful opportunity to make Kindness Hearts for Knit the Rainbow. Now the hearts were going places, and each person who received a handmade garment from Knit the Rainbow got one of those messages of kindness. Those tags have since been replaced with important information on resources for unhoused people, but I still make hearts for KtR, along with many other people.

Then came Vogue Knitting Live New York, and the tradition of giving out hearts directly to people began. When I put the Kindness Hearts on social media, I invited people to make their own hearts and share them in their parts of the world. People did. Kindness spread.

You can do this too. Kindness Hearts are small, but powerful. They touch people's hearts! They make people happy, but the happiest people are the ones giving them out.

Here's how you can get started with this fun and very necessary project. It's easy to make dozens of hearts while you're medKNITating or watching TV. The messages take a bit longer, but when you see the smiles and even tears of gratitude, you'll agree that they're well worth the time.

THE PATTERN

I searched for patterns for small hearts on YouTube and found my favorite, which is by Crochet Lovers, the English language version of Ahuyama Crochet. Look for "How to Crochet a HEART (tiny size)."

For a knitted heart, go to YouTube, search LoveCrafts, and look for "How to Knit The Fastest Heart." This is larger than the hearts I make, but size could be affected by yarn weight.

There are many other video tutorials and patterns all over the wide world of the world wide web. My suggestion is to try a few and stick with the one that's easiest. You may end up making a *lot* of these—I never thought I'd be in the thousands by now!—so you want a pattern that's quick, simple, and easy on your hands and fingers.

Whether you knit or crochet your hearts, leave a long tail of about eight inches at the beginning and another at the end. This is not specified in patterns or shown in tutorials, which generally advise snipping and hiding ends. By leaving long tails at the start and end, you'll have enough yarn to tie on your message tags, and so your recipient can tie their heart onto something.

WHAT YOU NEED TO MAKE KINDNESS HEARTS

Making Kindness Hearts is easy, super-fun, and doesn't cost much. As a stitcher, you'll already have some things on hand. Others are easy to get from a craft store or online. You'll need: yarn, knitting needles or crochet hook that work with the yarn weight, a scissor, tags for messages of kindness, and a pen (preferably with waterproof ink).

Yarn: I've found the yarn that's best for making Kindness Hearts is also the cheapest. The kind of yarn that doesn't have much stretch or softness means the hearts won't flop or look shapeless once knitted or crocheted; they'll stay true to their little heart form. Because I make so many hearts at a time, I get large skeins of inexpensive acrylic yarn (cotton yarn will work too, but it will cost more). I've been able to make over a hundred hearts from a skein that costs about five dollars (U.S.) or less. My favorite weight to use for making hearts is worsted weight, 7 oz./198 g., but you don't have to be exact with this. I just like the size of hearts this makes, but if you want larger or smaller, go for it with different weights of yarn. Tip: experiment with your scrap yarn before you buy loads of new yarn.

As for colors, my signature color is a sort of fuchsia that my Nana liked to call "shocking pink." I use rainbow yarn to make Rainbow Hearts for Pride events. Austin from Knit the Rainbow suggested that I get some yarn in pink, blue, and white to represent our transgender friends, and I found some online. Use whatever colors work for you, and for the people you intend to gift with hearts.

Tools: The knitting needles or crochet hook you use should work with the size of your yarn, though I experiment with that, too. I want to get a really tight stitch so the heart form takes shape, so I crochet much tighter than I normally would. Using smaller sizes of tools can also help with that, though ultimately you should use what feels most comfortable for you. You'll also need a scissor for snipping your yarn.

Message tags: Kindness Hearts say a lot on their own, but I've found they're even more powerful when you include a heartfelt message along with them. I use craft paper tags that measure 2 3/4 inches by 1 3/8 inches, preferably made from recycled paper. These are very small, so get larger ones if you feel that writing this small might be challenging. The tags should have a hole at the top so you can tie them on to your hearts.

Pen: I like to use pens with waterproof ink to reduce the chance of smearing. Craft paper tags have a bit of tooth (grain), and some pens will skip. I try to use fountain pens with non-water-soluble ink to reduce plastic waste as most plastic pens are not recyclable (at least in my area). If you need to use plastic pens, the Uniball Vision Rollerball pen has a good flow that works perfectly with craft paper tags. If you get non-craft paper tags that have a smoother surface, almost any pen will work for writing your kind messages.

WHAT SHOULD YOU WRITE ON THE TAGS?

People who've been inspired to join the Kindness Hearts Project have asked me what kind of messages they should write on the tags of their hearts. I have a few golden rules I follow that are inspired by one of my heroes, Fred Rogers of *Mr. Rogers' Neighborhood* fame. I grew up with Fred Rogers' kind approach on his PBS children's show, and his mission of kindness and inclusivity continues to be needed today. The Kindness Heart message guidelines I follow are:

- I say the kind words I would want to say to a child, such as: *You are wonderful. You have value beyond measure. You are a gift from the Universe. You are magic. You are made of stars. You are loved, and you are Love.*
- I like to remind people that they can spread kindness just by being themselves. *Your smile is your superpower. You make everyone you meet feel loved. You make this world a better place. Your heart radiates kindness.*
- I don't tell people what to do, not even that they should be more kind. I just remind them of their own essential goodness by writing *Everything about you is wonderful. You are the bloom of Love. You are a miracle. You are perfect just as you are. You are a blessing. You are the Universe's Valentine.*

Once you start writing from the heart, the words will come to you in a flurry of kindness.

"WHAT'S THIS FOR?"

Sometimes I'll give someone a heart, and although they're touched by the gift and the sentiment on the tag, they'll ask, "What's this for? What do I do with this?" The answer to the first question is, "It's for you!" But the answer to what they're really asking, what the heart is meant to do, is that it's first of all meant to share kindness in the world, one heart and one person at a time. In a more practical sense, you can use Kindness Hearts:

- as a bookmark
- tied to a project bag
- tied to a luggage handle for quick identification on a baggage carousel
- tied to a child's backpack, or your own
- attached to the zipper of your knitting tools bag
- added to your inspiration board, so you can see it every day
- put in a place with special mementos
- enclosed in a card you're giving to someone
- tied to a gift
- placed in a loved one's lunch bag
- tied to holiday decorations

I'm sure there are more things you can do with Kindness Hearts, but the most important ones are to make them and give them out!

JOIN THE KINDNESS HEARTS PROJECT

People may have their differences, but I think we can all agree that the world could use more kindness. Why not be the kind change you want to see in the world? Joining the Kindness Hearts Project is simple: make a bunch of hearts and give them out. Give them to kids, who will remember loving messages for the rest of their lives. Give them to adults, whose days and even lives can be changed by one small act of kindness. Give them to friends and strangers. Give them to teachers, hospital workers, postal and shipping delivery people.

Once in a blue moon, someone will say "No thank you," and I've even had people hand a heart back to me. That's okay; it just means the heart is meant to move on. I quietly wish the person well and look for the next person.

Mostly, what you'll get is a look of surprise, then a smile, and, occasionally, tears of gratitude. What you really get is the wonderful feeling of sharing kindness. The more kindness you give, the more joy you'll feel.

BINDING OFF, BEGINNING AGAIN

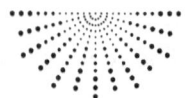

In meditation instruction, students are encouraged to have a "beginner's mind." This is the mental attitude of someone who is teachable, open to learning. If you go into something thinking you already know a lot about that particular subject, you're building walls against new experiences. Go in as a beginner, and you'll rarely be disappointed by whatever happens.

I've been practicing meditation for thirty years. I've received instruction in ashrams and Yoga studios and meditation centers. I've practiced at home, on trains, in office chairs and waiting room chairs. Each day, I sit to meditate, or try to, anyway. Each time, I come to meditation with a beginner's mind, because while I may know the directions to get where I want to go, I never know what's going to happen along the way. If I think I've got this, I close myself off to new experiences.

Had I not learned from wise teachers who practiced for decades and still came to each day with an open, teachable mindset, this book would not exist. Knitting would have been just knitting, something I did while watching TV and nothing more. I wouldn't have experienced the spiritual connection that comes when I make something with my hands in a quiet space. I wouldn't have recognized the similarities between the effects of meditation attained by traditional paths and the effects of knitting, crochet, and stitching. I wouldn't have sought out Dr. Carl Birmingham and heard him talk about the incredible, but scientifically measurable, effects knitting had on his patients in the eating disorder clinic. I wouldn't have been able to share that with people at medKNITation gatherings and lectures, and the people who listened wouldn't have told me afterward that knitting as their method of coping with anxiety now had validation, and that they felt empowered. "I knew I was right," said one person at the medKNITation lecture in 2020. "People told me that couldn't be true, knitting to calm my anxiety. Now I can tell them it's real."

That's what I wanted to tell you with this book: Yes, knitting as a form of meditation is real. The only way I was able to do that was by keeping the beginner's mindset.

People like to trust in certainty, but one of the things I hope to achieve through meditation is being able to trust in myself. To hear, as is said, the still, small voice within. I can only hear that voice by being a beginner every day and starting fresh.

At some point in each project, we bind off, our stitches signaling an ending. (Except, of course, for that pile of unfinished objects in the closet.) Then we begin another project. Even when we work with a pattern we know so well we can do it by heart, with yarn and tools as familiar as extensions of our own hands and fingers, each project is new. We cast on; we begin again. With each breath, we begin again.

We've come to the beginning of this project. Yes, the end of the book, though you can go back, like getting out that familiar pattern, and revisit meditations. Some of them you may have liked, some you may have needed, and some you may want in the future. Now, you have not only this book of meditations, but you also have a way to meditate. You know the pattern.

In a way, you always knew it.

Each knitting project is made of a series of continuing loops of yarn. Each of us is made of a series of breaths, and experiences, and stories—some meant to be repeated, others meant to be unraveled and repurposed—and with each new day, we begin again.

Rare is the project that doesn't teach you something new, about the yarn, about knitting, about yourself and where you are in life. No matter how long you've been knitting, no matter how many fancy shawls you've made and stitches you've learned, approach your knitting meditations with a beginner's mind. This will keep you fresh, willing, wild, quick to laugh, to weep when you need to and then take a deep breath, and be able to see what might be missed, hear what isn't spoken. Bring this attitude to your knitting meditations and it will be a friend to you wherever you go in life. Whether you're eleven or twenty-one or one hundred and one, with each new day, be a beginner. Begin again; begin anew.

Let's cast on and begin.

GRATITUDE LIST

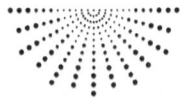

I want to start by thanking you, dear reader, because I wrote this book for you. We may never have met, but we're alike in that we both love knitting, and we both have lives that take us to different places, some beautiful, some challenging. My intention and hope with this book were that it would become a companion for you, broadening what knitting means to you, as it has for me. I'm grateful to you for joining me in this ever-growing knitting circle of kindness.

Writing is a solitary path, but I'm never alone. There are so many people who contributed to this book in various ways, by helping directly, by doing something that lit a candle in my mind, by teaching me, by telling me something that stayed in my heart, by giving me some gift that became part of this book.

First on this gratitude list is Knitty City, the yarn shop where the idea for medKNITation began and took shape. I give thanks to Pearl Chin, founder and matriarch of Knitty City, may she rest in power. She created a vibrant community that continues to thrive, thanks to her son Zac Chin. Thanks also to everyone who was so kind to me in the Knitty City community: Maxine Levinson, my knitting guru; Melissa Soong; the talented, caring people who work there to help people, and all those at the knitting table who invited me to sit with them. My

175

thanks to everyone I met during medKNITations at Knitty City for sharing the gift of your time and divine presence.

Through Knitty City I met Nancy Ricci, a person who exemplifies generosity of spirit, and one of those angels who introduces you to everyone as "My friend" even though you've only just met her. I'm grateful to call her my friend. Nancy introduced me to Carolyn Bloom, an ingenious stitching maestro who has that feel-good energy you can't get enough of. Together, we three meet, talk about life, and lift each other up.

As proof that yarn shops are houses of community, I met more wonderful friends through Knitty City: Tanya Singer, who called me one day and said, "Yarn Crawl. I'm picking you up in an hour." Cecilia Nelson-Hurt, who gave a wonderful lecture on inclusivity by using different colored balls of yarn, and who would later recommend me to give meditation sessions at Vogue Knitting Live. And Louis Boria, who, when he became a social media sensation overnight, showed us that if a person wants to be good, they *do* good.

One of Louis's good-doing missions was teaching hospital staff and patients how to de-stress through knitting. Through that joyful event, I met Alexis Mantione, the genius behind My Two Ladies knitting and crochet tools and someone who takes time out of her outrageously busy day just to say she thinks you're great. Alexis introduced me to Stacy Wiener, whose Soap S.A.C.K. project you read about in this book, so you know how she inspires people.

I give gratitude to Vogue Knitting Live's Gabrielle Ald, who took a chance on a knitting meditation thing she'd heard about, first making it a lecture, and then a regular part of VKL's online offerings. To this day, people tell me how much those morning meditations meant during the pandemic, and that was Gabby's idea.

People who are invited to give classes at Vogue Knitting Live New York attend a teachers' meeting before the event begins. Everyone there seemed to know each other; I, a relatively new knitter who taught meditation, knew nobody. I sat alone until Mary Jane Mucklestone said to her friend Gudrun Johnston, "Let's sit here," indicating the chairs next to me. They introduced themselves, asked me what I was teaching, and brought me into the group. One small gesture, one big act of kindness. Friends, if you see someone sitting alone, go say hi.

At VKL, I saw a stunning art exhibit that showed me the power of crochet as an art medium. The artist: London Kaye, who also happened to be a kind and encouraging person. Though she barely knew me, she always had the right words to make this doubter have faith in my work. The same can be said of Josh Bennett, who listened to a seed of an idea I had and turned it into sunflowers—the ones that became my Heart of Ukraine project for VKL. These two showed me how people in the fiber community support each other.

To the one hundred and sixty-plus people who came to that first medKNITation lecture at Vogue Knitting Live, thank you. To everyone who came to the virtual medKNITations, you have my gratitude. You are all, in person or online, in my heart.

I used to work at the *Oprah* Magazine, and I'd always thought of Modern Daily Knitting as being a yarn-centric extension of *O*. One day, I took a chance and asked/begged to write an article for MDK. I thank Kay Gardiner, Ann Shayne, Cristina Shiffman, and Adrienne Martini for letting me join their group of talented contributors. I'm honored.

There are so many other people who, in their own ways, contributed to this book: Carol Caparosa, founder of Project Knitwell; artist and exemplar of integrity Lorna Hamilton Brown; Felicia Eve of String Thing Studio, who has a smile for everyone; Cat Bordhi, who gave the gift of knitting to countless children in her lifetime; Melanie Falick, who showed me the deeper meaning of handcrafts; Clara Parkes, who puts the heart of fiber arts to words; and Dr. Carl Birmingham, a true believer in the power of knitting. Your work continues to empower knitters.

My agent, Jill Marsal of Marsal Lyon Literary Agency, believed in this book, and she tried to find a home for it; thank you, Jill, for always listening to my ideas. My lifelong friend David Keeps told me that our mutual friend, Michael Dolan, had launched a publishing imprint called Winding Road Stories. Michael's beloved mother, Julie Dolan, was a knitter. He understands the deep meaning of the handmade, and he understood why this book had to be. I am so grateful to him, and to the WRDS team.

I'm forever grateful to my friend Donna Herman for asking me if I'd like to try knitting lessons with her, and to our teacher Susan for making what might have been frustrating fun.

The drawings I did throughout this book, and the ones I do for myself, are thanks to Danny Gregory, JJ Gregory, and my dear friend Koosje Koene, all from Sketchbook Skool. They all helped to make art a part of my life again.

I can't find the right or rich enough words to say thank you to Alice Uniman for her wisdom and kindness, but: thank you.

To my family, my sisters Laurie, Mandy, Luisa, and Becky; my stepmothers Sheila and Ruth; my brother Adam, sister-in-law Kristi, nephews Calder, Lachlan, Eirnan, Seth, and Evan; my niece Olivia and brother-in-law Daryl: I love you all.

Anyone who has an animal friend knows of unconditional love. I've been blessed with many rescue cats over the years, and the two who sat by my side while I wrote and knitted are Norman and Sherman. They occasionally play with my yarn and make kitty biscuits in my knits; small price to pay for the love they make me feel.

My parents, Carolyn and David, are indescribably wonderful, immeasurably supportive, wise, *and* funny. Without them, nothing; with them, everything.

And to Nathan, the love of my life, the husband who says, "Hey, there's a yarn shop—want to check it out?", who tied hundreds of messages onto my Kindness Hearts, who makes the world a better place every chance he gets, who makes me a better person each day because I get to love him. Thank you, my love.

ABOUT THE AUTHOR

Suzan Colón is the author of *Cherries in Winter: My Family's Recipe for Hope in Hard Times*, *Yoga Mind: Journey Beyond the Physical: 30 Days to Enhance Your Practice and Revolutionize Your Life from the Inside Out*, and *Beach Glass*, a novel. Suzan is a former Senior Editor of *O, the Oprah Magazine* and has appeared on *Good Morning America*, *CBS's Early Show*, NPR, and other media outlets. Suzan trained at Integral Yoga Institute of New York to teach Yoga and meditation in Hatha Yoga Levels I and II, Yoga for Arthritis, and other specialized Yoga programs. Suzan has also taught meditation through drawing for Sketchbook Skool and the Sktchy app. For more information and to subscribe to Suzan's newsletter, please visit suzancolon.net and suzancolon.substack.com.

www.ingramcontent.com/pod-product-compliance
Lightning Source LLC
Chambersburg PA
CBHW031517120626
46545CB00005B/1910